051967

Class, Race
and Sport
in South Africa's
Political
Economy

Class, Race and Sport in South Africa's Political Economy

Grant Jarvie

Routledge & Kegan Paul
London, Boston, Melbourne and Henley

First published in 1985
by Routledge & Kegan Paul plc

14 Leicester Square, London WC2H 7PH, England

9 Park Street, Boston, Mass. 02108, USA

464 St Kilda Road, Melbourne,
Victoria 3004, Australia and

Broadway House, Newtown Road,
Henley on Thames, Oxon RG9 1EN, England

Set in 10 on 12 point Imprint
and printed in Great Britain
by Butler & Tanner Ltd,
Frome and London

Library of Congress Cataloging in Publication Data

Jarvie, Grant, 1955–

Class, race, and sport in South Africa's political
economyBibliography: p.
Includes index.
1. *Sport and state—South Africa.* 2. *South Africa—*
Race relations. 3. *South Africa—Social policy.*
I. Title
GV706.8.J37   1985   305'.89068   84–18096

British Library CIP data also available

ISBN 0–7102–0443–4

For Margaret, David and Colin

CONTENTS

Preface and acknowledgments   vii

Abbreviations   ix

Introduction   1

1   THE THEORETICAL FRAMEWORK   7
2   A HERITAGE OF STRUGGLE   25
3   THE POLITICAL ECONOMY OF WHITE SPORTING PRACTICE   44
4   SPORT AND RESISTANCE   64
5   CONCLUSIONS   78

APPENDIX 1:   South African disputes involving black workers at the height of the 1981 strike wave   83

APPENDIX 2:   The South African government's official multinational sports policy   86

APPENDIX 3:   South African sporting history   88

Notes   91
Bibliography   97
Index   103

PREFACE AND ACKNOWLEDGMENTS

It is undeniable that changes have taken place in South Africa. P.W. Botha came into office promising reforms in apartheid. Yet the script is grim, and the historic logic that informs it raises alarm. The current reforms pre-suppose the entire apartheid system and only attempt to make the system of repression and exploitation more efficient. It is often forgotten that the changes that have been made by the apartheid regime were staffed and implemented by its own supporters to deal with its own crises. Recent examples are no different in that they only serve to reinforce the lessons learned from history.

I am grateful to a number of people for their comments, encouragement and advice. Hart Cantelon, Aniko Varpalotai, Elia Zureik and the Queen's University crew provided much intellectual stimulus and friendship during the 1981–2 period. I would also like to thank Colin Leys for his constructive criticism and Sam Ramsamy and Richard Lapchick for proving to be invaluable sources of information. Special thanks must also go to Rita Ford, Jim Fegley, Peter Hopkins and Elizabeth Taylor. Above all I am indebted to Rick Gruneau, who ruined my summer by asking for editorial changes all of which greatly improved the text, and to Andi Farbman who not only provided a home in a number of counties but also cast a critical eye over the manuscript. My gratitude to everyone. I hope the result justifies their efforts.

Needless to say, I am ultimately responsible for the final form this book has taken.

The author and publishers are grateful to Zed Books for permission to reprint material from *The South African Game:*

ABBREVIATIONS

ANC	African National Congress
AZAPO	Azanian African People's Organisation
BAD	Department of Bantu Administration and Development
BCAWU	Black and Allied Workers' Union
BCM	Black Consciousness Movement
BOSS	Bureau for State Security
FCWU	Food and Canning Workers' Union
FOSATU	Federation of South African Trade Unions
GWU	Garment Workers' Union
ICU	Industrial Commercial Workers' Union
IOC	International Olympic Committee
MAWU	Motor Assembly Workers' Union
MWU	Mine Workers' Union
NUMARW	National Union of Motor Assembly and Rubber Workers
OAU	Organisation of African Unity
PAC	Pan Africanist Congress
SACOS	South African Council on Sport
SACP	South African Communist Party
SACTU	South African Congress of Trade Unions
SADF	South African Defence Force
SAN-ROC	South African Non-Racial Olympic Committee
SAP	South African Police
SASA	South African Sports Association
SASO	South African Student Organisation
TUCOSA	Trade Union Council of South Africa

INTRODUCTION

By means of sport, a new dimension is being given to
our policy of multi-nationalism and to the South
African set up, which, since 1652, has been in
embryo what it has become today. We should not
lose sight of the fact that we are dealing with an
historic situation. Sport is being used to create a
spirit and attitude which have a positive value, a
spirit and attitude which are giving new dimensions
to our multi-national set up (Minister of Sport and
Recreation, *Hansard*, 18 May 1977).

Over the last two decades there has been considerable interest
in the patterns and policies of South African sport.[1] The expulsion of South Africa from the Olympics, struggles over
touring South African teams such as the cricket tour of Britain
in the early 1970s and the more recent Zola Budd affair[2] have
all served to focus international attention on South Africa's
sports policy. On the one hand a number of writers have argued that South African sport has been liberalised, while, on
the other, some have suggested that sport remains a mechanism
for the extension of apartheid policy in general. Most of these
writers have tended to focus their evaluations purely on the
question of race and have thereby missed the complex interaction between racial and class dynamics as a background for
understanding the South African sporting way of life.

In this study I propose to redress this imbalance by using
the concepts of class conflict, ideology and cultural struggle as
axial principles for analysing the nature, meaning and political
significance of South African sports policy. Within this broad

1

frame of reference this study has two inter-related emphases: (1) to demonstrate that sport must not be understood abstractly or simply in the context of ideas about racial prejudice, but rather in the context of the ensemble of social relations characterising the South African social formation; (2) to suggest the significance of sport as a field of cultural struggle in the overall resistance to South African ruling hegemony. In order to clarify these objectives it is necessary to devote a part of this introduction to a more detailed explanation of the frame of reference to be used in this study.

A framework for analysis

The complex interaction of racial and class dynamics in South Africa has often been concealed by the appearance of social realities under apartheid. Race and racial discrimination appear to be the dominant consideration determining and affecting all aspects of social life. Black people, regardless of class position, are systematically denied equality of opportunity in political, economic and cultural spheres. Yet what this overlooks is the fact that South African racism has not evolved in a social vacuum. Rather it has developed in conjunction with very significant relations of colonisation, capitalist development and western imperialism.

It is along these lines that the South African Congress of Trade Unions ruled in 1962[3] that:

> It must never be forgotten that apartheid and racial
> discrimination in South Africa, like everywhere else,
> has an aim far more important than discrimination
> itself; the aim is economic exploitation. The root and
> fruit of apartheid and racial discrimination is profit.

The argument being made here is that South Africa can be understood with regard to the production process and the social relationships formed around the mode of production. Rather than analyse racial discrimination solely in terms of political or ideological structures, any particular racial system can also be examined as a specific set of social relations generated by a particular capitalist mode of production.

2

Building on these ideas I shall argue in this study that the main characteristics of South African society may be summarised as follows. Firstly, it is a capitalist social formation in which the mass of the population have been separated from the means of production and where the production of commodities is greatly dependent upon cheap labour, foreign exchange, and western investment. Secondly, and uniquely, the overwhelming majority of the population, including most of the industrial working class, is denied, both in law and in fact, many civil and political rights on the grounds of colour. In the 1970s and 1980s, however, many Africans have enjoyed a less stringent implementation of several petty apartheid rules. To understand these concessions in the context of the historical process, it is necessary, I believe, to consider what Gramsci refers to as an organic crisis (Gramsci, 1980: 175).

The process of capital accumulation in South Africa during the 1970s has led to certain structural tensions, which have underpinned the crisis which has broken out over the last decade. In a statement to journalists, Harry Oppenheimer, Chairman of South Africa's largest single business enterprise, warned of possible revolution in white minority South Africa unless blacks get major concessions soon.[4] Furthermore, events in Durban 1972, Soweto 1976, Johannesburg 1980 and Sasolburg 1980 have amply demonstrated that it is not necessary merely to hypothesise the presence of revolutionary energy in South Africa – it is there. This current, living crisis in South Africa is what Gramsci (1980: 177–8) referred to as an organic crisis:

> A crisis occurs, sometimes lasting for decades. This exceptional duration means that incurable structural contradictions have revealed themselves (reached maturity) and that despite this, the political forces that are struggling to conserve and defend the existing structure itself are making every effort to cure them, within certain limits, and to overcome them.

At the core of Gramsci's model of transformation is a dual perspective involving the organic and conjunctural dimensions of change. By conjunctural Gramsci meant the passing and

3

momentary period of a crisis during which the contesting political forces struggle for state power. As Hall (1981) points out, the conjunctural must be seen in terms of a lived historical bloc in which new political configurations, new programmes and new policies point to a new settlement. The conjunctural does not merely emerge but is constructed by the dominant culture and, as such, it must be seen as part of the dominant ideology. The organic, on the other hand, must precede the conjunctural. A crisis occurs when structural contradictions occur within the organic. As such, the conjunctural must not be seen as a reflection of the crisis but as a response to it.

It is entirely appropriate to see much of this as directly applicable to the current situation in South Africa. The process of capital accumulation which has evolved historically in South Africa entered a period of crisis during the 1970s, with the emergence of a skilled white labour shortage and a periodic slump in the price of gold. Yet such events alone are not enough to term the crisis facing the South African social formation as organic. A transformation of this nature resulted from the dramatic escalation in resistance to apartheid rule from the number of oppressed cultural groupings. In short, the organic crisis in this study revolves around two key dimensions: firstly, the structural contradictions which have emerged from the process of capital accumulation and increased the dependency of the white minority culture upon the African majority; secondly, the increase in resistance as exemplified by the events leading up to and after Soweto.

The conjunctural dimension to the crisis refers to the attempts being made by the current policy decision-makers to introduce a number of new programmes and policies aimed at maintaining important features of the status quo. If transformation of a broader nature is going to take place it is precisely this dominant cultural response that the forces of opposition must organise against. In any case, accounts of social change in general must not only allow for structural limits to change but also the ways in which such limits are dealt with by subordinate groups and cultures. Related to this is the important issue of how subordinate groups try to penetrate and resist the dominant culture.

It is within the area of the conjunctural that one can understand the significance of the struggle over South Africa's sport-

4

ing policies. Very few areas of reform have been more widely publicised by the white government than its 'multinational sports programme', first introduced in 1971, but only widely publicised since 1977. As Dr Koornhof, Minister of Sport and Recreation, noted in 1977:

> Let us admit here this afternoon that play and sport are strong enough to cause political and economic relations to flourish or collapse. (*Hansard*, 18 May 1977)

Through considering some of the economic and political issues surrounding sport, the South African sporting policy can be seen for what it really is, no more than a facelift, part of the ideology of reform constructed by the dominant culture in response to a growing crisis. As such, sporting policy can be seen to be part of the dominant ideology which supports apartheid. Since coming to power in 1978, Botha[5] has continually insisted that a real effort would be made to make things inside the country seem better. The most visible areas of South African life were to be improved and, to this end, some of the peripheral edges of apartheid could be eroded for public visibility. The peripheral edges chosen were sport and recreation. Thus reform in sport became a major element of the *verligtes*'[6] apartheid policy. The *verligtes*' approach is based on the reasoning that a black revolution can be averted by opening certain doors to the aspirant black middle class and negotiating away all but the core of apartheid.

In evaluating current 'reforms' concerning South African sport I shall attempt to dismantle the ideology surrounding multinational sport, trace the struggle for black recognition in non-racial sport, and assess the way in which sport, in its limited sense, is being used to bring pressure to bear on South Africa, both internally and externally. It is precisely the value which the white dominant culture places on sport that makes cultural struggle in the area of sport an important part of movements towards resistance and liberation. For example, commenting on the political strategy of sports isolation that has been pursued since 1970, Helen Suzman, Member of Parliament, has stated:

This is the only thing that really hurts South
Africans where they feel it. (*Hansard*, 22 April 1971)

In order to address these themes, I have organised my work
into five chapters. Chapter 1 is essentially theoretical in that it
considers the weaknesses of some of the traditional approaches
to race relations (see Banton, 1967; Kuper and Smith, 1969;
Van den Berghe, 1967, 1969) and contrasts these with a Marxist analysis of South Africa (Magubane, 1979; Stasiulis, 1980;
Adam, 1971, 1979). Instead of providing an historical liberal
account, it is argued that South Africa must ultimately be
understood in terms of the changing social relationships
formed around the mode of production. Having argued for a
historical materialist frame of reference in Chapter 1, Chapter
2 switches to a more specific analysis of South Africa. An
attempt is made to link elements of Marxian social and political
theory as the basis for understanding aspects of social change
taking place in South African society today (Callinicos, 1981;
Saul and Gelb, 1981; Seidman, 1980. Hirson, 1979).

Together Chapters 1 and 2 provide the background for con-
ducting an analysis of South African sports policy that emphasises the significance of class conflict and ideological struggle. This analysis is developed in Chapters 3 and 4 with
specific reference to sport's role as part of the conjunctural,
ideological bloc constructed by white dominant culture. Chapter 3 documents the history of white sporting policy and the
development of multiracial sport and includes a critique of
dominant forms of sporting practice. Chapter 4 looks at the
history of non-racial sporting organisations in South Africa
and the extent to which sport, in particular black sport, might
be used as part of a total strategy in fighting racial and class
domination, both internally and externally. Finally, Chapter 5
provides a summary and concluding statement to the argu-
ments and issues raised in this book.

ONE

THE THEORETICAL FRAMEWORK

Until recently, analyses of South African race relations have been heavily dependent upon the notion of pluralism. In this chapter I want to review some of the criticisms of South African apartheid policy that have developed out of the pluralist framework. I shall then develop the argument that a Marxist perspective which addresses the question of being and consciousness as central features of class relations is able to generate a clearer understanding of the South African situation.

The pluralist framework

Just as a society can be segmented horizontally, so too can it be segmented vertically. The tradition of a plural society in the study of race relations often takes as its starting point the work of two authors, namely Furnivall and Smith. The term pluralism was first used by Furnivall in reference to colonial countries. In *Colonial Policy and Practice* (1948) he uses the term to refer to situations in which different ethnic groups keep to themselves but are under the domination of the same polity and are forced to trade in the same market situation. This type of pluralism is termed 'social pluralism'.

On the other hand, Smith prefers to use the term 'cultural pluralism' (Smith, 1960). He noted that the term refers to a general theory of society and therefore is not limited to societies divided on racial and ethnic lines. It therefore could be applied to societies divided on the basis of social class or religion, etc. However, in practice, Smith restricted his use of the term 'cultural pluralism' to refer to specific types of

7

societies. Firstly, he uses the term to refer to societies where a cultural minority was dominant and the only unifying factor was that of a coercive political institution. Secondly, he restricted the use of the term to societies where institutional differentiation was complete (with the exception of the political sphere), i.e. sections having different kinship, economies, education, etc. There is in this case, Smith argues, a duplication of institutions within one society which implies cultural differentiation (Smith, 1960: 761).

In general agreement with Smith, Van den Berghe argues that the notion of pluralism used by Smith is too restricted (Van den Berghe, 1967). Societies are pluralistic in so far as they are segmented into different groups that frequently, although not necessarily, have different outlines or subcultures. Plural societies, according to Van den Berghe, have a number of characteristics, such as a relative absence of value consensus, relative absence of conflict between groups, political domination by one of the groups over the others and a relative presence of cultural heterogeneity (Van den Berghe, 1967). For instance, it can be argued from this perspective that different societies have varying degrees of pluralism. South Africa divided into four major racial castes and several different cultural traditions is more pluralistic than the United States which has two major castes (black and white), who share the same esteem, culture and language. It is to the South African situation that I now specifically want to turn.

A number of pluralistic analyses of South Africa have been undertaken by a number of authors such as Kuper, Louw and Van den Berghe, to name but a few. The latter in various works, notably *South Africa: A Study in Conflict* (1965), *Race and Racism* (1967) and *Race and Ethnicity* (1969) has argued that:

> South Africa is probably the most complex and the most conflict-ridden of the world's multi-racial societies. The most salient lines of clevage are those of race. (324)

The basic tenet of Van den Berghe's analysis is that of all the contemporary multiracial societies, South Africa is the most complex in that it is rigidly stratified on the basis of race.

Race, it is argued, has the greatest salience vis-à-vis other structural principles and it is on the basis of race that South Africa is the most modern multiracial society ridden with conflict and internal contradictions. Consensus, it is argued, is almost totally absent in a South Africa which is held together in a state of what Van den Berghe calls 'static disequilibrium' through political coercion and economic dependence.

One invariant feature of pluralism, other than the emphasis on race, has been the view that plural societies represent but one stage in the progress of undeveloped countries to advanced capitalism. For instance Van den Berghe (1965: 212) asserts that with the exception of a reactionary political structure South African society has behaved in a similar fashion to any economy in transition from underdevelopment to industrialisation.

To summarise, the pluralist writing on South Africa has been characterised firstly by a preoccupation with race and racial ideology and secondly by what might be referred to as institutional determinism.[1] Within this framework the South African social formation is polarised into two components: (1) the capitalist economic system which is seen as functional, harmonious and totally integrated; (2) a system of political domination based on a racial ideology which is seen as dysfunctional.

Opponents of the pluralist scenario have criticised pluralist accounts as failing to analyse the underlying structural causes of apartheid's continuity and success. In moving towards a Marxist analysis of South Africa it is necessary, I believe, to consider first of all some of the major criticisms of the pluralist framework.

The critique of pluralism

Criticisms of pluralism stem from two main sources. The first of these might be called the 'liberal critique' and is symbolised by the work of Heribert Adam. This approach pinpoints a number of material and political forces as having primacy over explanations revolving around race and ethnicity. The second critique derives from Marxism and emphasises the significance of class domination and class struggle in the analyses of South African society.

9

In *Modernising Racial Domination* Adam (1971) outlines the liberal political and economic viewpoint. While agreeing with the pluralists that apartheid has incurred great wastes when measured in terms of individual productivity Adam criticises Kuper, Van den Berghe and other pluralists for not questioning the reasons for racial conflict and diversity as the outcome of a continual struggle over scarce resources. Economic development has proceeded in South Africa despite the existence of racist legislation, not because of it. Furthermore, on the future of the system of white supremacy Adam rejects the pluralists' assumption that economic growth will erase racial discrimination. But, at the same time, Adam is not willing to concede that economic development is at all compatible with white supremacy in the long run. This is based on the assumption that the shortage of white skilled labour and an unstable labour force in the 1970s has increased the dependency of the white population upon non-white labour and consequently increased the power base of the African.

The continued existence of apartheid lies in the pragmatic manipulation of policy decisions which subordinate ideological considerations to national changes which maintain the privileges of a few whites at the expense of the majority. South Africa is referred to by Adam in terms of a 'pragmatic racial oligarchy'. While the South African government attempts to keep the traditional power structure and ideology of apartheid alive, it also recognises in the face of external pressure that some form of modification is necessary if the system is to survive. In its present form two major forces hold South African society together. The first of these is a common participation by all cultures in an industrialised economy and therefore a certain degree of economic interdependence. The second force is the coercion of the state under the control of the white master race.

Pragmatism, Adam goes on, overrides many explanations stemming from racial attitudes and is oriented solely towards the smooth, frictionless control of cheap labour as a basis for political domination. This type of system is seen as pragmatic in the sense that all dissidents and political opponents are silenced through a repressive state apparatus. The system and network of police surveillance has been improved and modernised, to such an extent that it alone guarantees an effective

10

check on all opponents inside and outside the country. Any analysis, it is argued, which focuses only on the repressive aspects of the South African system overlooks the new elements of the pragmatic oligarchy, such as the partial successes of the programme of separate development.

Taken as a whole, I believe that Adam's basic position can be summarised in the following passages:

1　If one is not to presuppose inherent aggressive tendencies among members of different racial stock, then the struggle for scarce resources among segmented groups has to be seen as the decisive reason for ethnic strife. (1971: 22)

2　Apartheid can best be understood as the systematic attempt to reverse economic integration as much as possible by legislating social barriers, in order to channel the inevitable political consequences of African economic advancement in the interests of the privileged whites. (1971: 8)

3　This study attempts to show that revolutionary change in South Africa . . . is unlikely to occur in the near future. (1971: 15)

4　Pragmatic racial oligarchy . . . overrides the ideological implications of racial beliefs and is oriented solely towards . . . tolerable domination over cheap labour and political dependents. (1971: 53)

Adam's analysis is a major advance over the pluralist perspective because it outlines the complex and dialectical nature of economic and political forces that underlies South African capitalism and the apartheid system. Yet there are still major weaknesses in Adam's thesis. These lie in two related areas. Firstly, he overlooks important differences between Afrikaner capitalism and South African capitalism as a whole. Secondly, as with the pluralist perspective, the part played by the black working class is relegated to that of a background feature. Yet it is of fundamental importance, I believe, to examine the degree to which the political and economic struggles among the different social groups in South Africa are in fact class struggles. That is, to examine the extent to which the struggles experienced by the white, and particularly the black, working classes arise from the relations of production. Instead of abstracting this or that feature of racial discrimination and explaining it in terms of other racial concepts, deemed as flowing from ideological and political structures, the South African situation must also be examined as a specific set of social relations characterised by the capitalist mode of production. The perspective which facilitates such an approach is a Marxist perspective.

A number of writers[2] have offered an analysis of South Africa in Marxist terms. These writers argue that the shortcomings of both the pluralist and liberal analysis is the tendency to treat all social cleavage and conflicts as race relations in the South African context. The advantage of class analysis is that it offers a more complex scenario which not only considers the conflict between races but also conflict within specific racial categories. The Marxist approach to the study of racially divided societies departs from the pluralist thesis in beginning its analysis not from the political or ideological levels, but rather from the study of any social formation in terms of the forces and relations of production which constitute any particular mode of production.

As Engels (1980: 417) indicates, Marx's materialist conception of history:

> starts from the proposition that the production of the means to support human life and, next to production, the exchange of things produced, is the basis of all social structure.

In fact, Marxism seeks to provide a scientific view of the world rooted in the analysis of the production and reproduction of the conditions of life. In the study of capitalism such an analysis involves a focus on social relationships which arise out of a fundamental division between the owners of capital and those who only have their labour to sell. This fundamental division, for Marx, formed the basis of class conflict and social structure in capitalistic societies.

In recent years the Marxist opponents of the pluralist and liberal approaches to the study of South Africa have offered a reinterpretation of South African development. Firstly, Wolpe (1972) has argued that apartheid cannot be seen merely as a reflection of a racial ideology nor can it be reduced to a single historical extension of segregation. Racial ideology, it is argued, must be seen as an ideology which sustains and reproduces capitalist relations of production. Secondly, Legassick (1974) has argued that the authoritarian and racially discriminatory South African social structure can only be explained in terms of specific historical processes of capital accumulation, e.g. the pervasiveness of the system of racial differentiation in the division of labour, the disparity between white affluence and black poverty, and the continual decline in African living standards. More recently Magubane (1979) has shown how racist legislation, in particular, has been shown to be integral to capitalist relations of production and functional in the processes of capital accumulation. Moreover Magubane's (1979: xi) historical analysis has led him to conclude that the struggle of the oppressed African people is not reversible:

> It is more evident now than ever before that South Africa's white supremacist state can neither regain the lost historical initiative nor reverse current developments.

It is often suggested that Marx's materialist perspective overtly values economic determinations and does not allow for the role of human agency in history-making. There is a great debate in contemporary political theory about the extent to which Marxism is economic determinism and I shall not digress into this debate here. I shall only say, following Raymond Williams (1976: 100), that Marx's conception of production can be thought of as a much broader conception of human activity than simple economics.

Similarly, there is in Marxism a great attempt to find a balance between the powers of human agents and the constraints imposed upon them by social relations. For example, in *The Eighteenth Brumaire of Louis Bonaparte*, Marx wrote:

> Men make their own history but they do not make it just as they please: they do not make it under circumstances chosen by themselves, but under

13

circumstances directly encountered, given and transmitted from the past. (Marx and Engels, 1980: 97)

It is this inter-linking between the freedom to make history
and the constraints imposed by various forms of human practice that is the central tenet of historical materialism.

To sum up it can be said that until recently work on South
African race relations has been heavily dependent upon pluralist and liberal frames of reference. Pluralist analyses that are
based on consensus, harmony and integration make the case
that race is the basis for a functional system of stratification.
Yet this approach fails to answer satisfactorily certain questions: it fails to explain the forces that are currently at work
restructuring social relations in the South African social formation; it fails to consider the extent to which the conflict that
has emerged within and between each social group is an en-
demic feature of the social formation rather than a temporary
and dysfunctional phase in development; it therefore fails to
provide an adequate model for social change because it simply
assumes that growth will reduce forms of racial discrimination.

A more critical but still liberal perspective, as in Adam's
work, provides a major advancement over the pluralist scenario
in that it pinpoints a number of material and political forces as
being central to any analysis of South Africa. Yet this, too,
fails to provide a satisfactory framework. Firstly, it fails to
highlight the advancements made by the working class.
Secondly, it fails to consider the development of consciousness
among various oppressed cultures in South Africa. Thirdly,
like the pluralist framework, it fails to provide an adequate
explanation of class conflict in the face of affluence.

The attraction of a Marxist perspective in the analysis of
South Africa is that it takes as its fundamental point of departure precisely that which seems missing in pluralist and liberal
analysis. That is, the struggle over the means of production,
the inevitability of conflict in capitalism, and the changing nature of class relations in history.

Yet it is essential to avoid deterministic or class reductionist
explanations of South Africa. In order to suggest how this
might be accomplished it is necessary to outline a less reductionist Marxist perspective.

Class struggle and cultural production

For Marx, every type of society, whether it be ancient, feudal or bourgeois, revolved around a mode of production. In the Marxist sense, the term bourgeois referred to a description of a type of society and the term capitalist to a description of a particular mode of production (Williams, 1981: 44). Each production system involves a different set of social relationships which in their totality denote a specific stage of development in the history of mankind. Thus:

> The social relations within which individuals
> produce, the social relations of production, change,
> are transformed with the change and development of
> the material means of production, in the productive
> forces. The relations of production in their totality
> constitute what are called the social relations of
> society, and specifically a society at a definite stage of
> historical development. (Marx and Engels, 1980: 81)

Capitalism then represents a specific stage in social development. Some of the characteristics, which are inherent in the capitalist set of social relations of production, include the accumulation of profit, surplus value and the process of commodity exchange. All the products which make up this specific set of social relations are in fact commodities. Capital therefore is not only the sum of material products, but the sum of commodities of exchange value. As Kidd points out, under capitalism more and more goods and services have been produced as commodities for exchange (Kidd, 1978: 7).

One such commodity is the labour power of the worker. Because the majority of people living in capitalist societies have no access or control over the means of production, in order to survive they must sell their labour power. The worker, in return for this labour power, receives the means of subsistence. What the worker actually receives is only a part of the whole from the accumulated productive activity which the capitalist receives in return. The development of surplus value and profit is one of the axial principles around which capitalism revolves.

A further prerequisite of the capitalist mode of production is the existence of a class which possesses nothing but the

15

capacity to labour. While in modern capitalist societies class relations may be subdivided into a number of dominant and subordinate fragments and subcultural formations, Marx initially identified two fundamental classes, namely the bourgeoisie and the proletariat.

These two classes in the capitalist social formation symbolised the fundamental conflict, inherent in the structure of the society, between those who owned the means of production and those who were subject to it. As Giddens asserts, in capitalist society classes are constituted by the relationship of groupings of individuals to the ownership of private property and capital in the means of production (Giddens, 1980: 37). This provides a basic model of class relations based on productive activity in which one group is dominant and the other subordinate.

There is danger, however, as Williams points out, in viewing class relations purely in terms of an economic category. While owners and wage-earners may be considered as economic categories, the main tendency in Marx's description of classes was towards a recognition of class and social formations. As Marx (cited in Williams, 1976: 58) puts it:

> That separate individuals form a class only insofar as
> they have to carry on a common battle against
> another class; otherwise they are on hostile terms
> with each other as competitors. On the other hand,
> the class in its turn achieves an independent existence
> over and against the individuals, so that the latter
> find their conditions of existence predestined, and
> hence have their position in life and their personal
> development assigned to them by their class.

The difficulty, writes Williams, is that while a class may be sometimes seen as an economic category, a class is often a social formation in which, for historical reasons, consciousness of the class situation has developed. Thus, in *The Eighteenth Brumaire of Louis Bonaparte* (from Williams, 1976: 59) Marx wrote:

> Insofar as millions of families live under economic
> conditions of existence that separate their mode of

life, their interests and their culture from those of the
other classes and put them in hostile opposition to
the latter, they form a class. Insofar as there is
merely a local interconnection among these
smallholding peasants, and the identity of their
interests begets no community . . . they do not form a
class.

There is a distinction then to be made between category and
formation. In the sense that the term class can swing between
the two meanings, it is useful to introduce the term 'culture'
or 'class culture'. For instance, working-class culture can refer
to the meanings, values, institutions of the formation, or the
tastes and life-style of the category (Williams, 1976: 59). Thus,
the value of the term 'culture' is summed up by Williams
(1976: 59) when he says:

The variations in meaning and reference, in the use
of culture, as a term, must be seen, I am arguing, not
simply as a disadvantage, which prevents any kind of
neat exclusion or definition, but as a genuine
complexity corresponding to real elements of
experience.

Culture is not just the way in which social relations of a
group or class are structured and shaped but also the way in
which these shapes are experienced,[3] understood and inter-
preted. Such a definition allows for a dynamic part to be played
by the subject within certain constrained limits. The shaping
of societies and the shaping of human minds is probably the
effective origin of the general sense of the term 'culture'. The
term, writes Williams, is taken a step further by the philoso-
pher Herder who pointed out that it was necessary to speak of
cultures and not 'culture' (Williams, 1977: 17). Therefore the
idea of a fundamental social process, which shapes specific and
distinctive ways of life, is the effective origin of the specific
comparative social sense of culture and its plural cultures.

The laws of social relations and the laws of culture are seen
by several writers to be one and the same thing. These structures not only shape the cohesive existence of groups, but also
constrain how these groups reproduce their own social exist-

17

ence. Whereas each individual group may be free to make its own history, it is only in so far as a particular culture, i.e. the dominant culture, limits the process. Each individual group makes the most of its own starting positions 'not under circumstances chosen by themselves' as Marx might put it, but under circumstances directly encountered, given and transmitted from the past. In considering any historical process, culture is a useful concept in that, through what Williams refers to as dominant, residual and emergent forms, it embodies the trajectory of group life through history.

Just as groups and classes are stratified in relation to one another, so too are cultures. Not only do dominant and subordinate cultures identify antagonistic interests, but subsets or subcultures within each parent culture, through entering into negotiation with the dominant and subordinate culture, also affect the process of change and the eventual outcome. In this way, the social formation of any society can be viewed as a dynamic, all-encompassing whole, constructed from many struggling, antagonistic, conflicting cultures and subcultures. In relations of domination and subordination, the determining factor is the degree of cultural power which a particular culture has. The struggle over social relationships is always a continual struggle over the distribution of cultural power, a continual struggle in which the dominant culture exerts a hegemony over subordinate cultures.

Hegemony and class struggle: a note on Gramsci's Marxism

From the start, it should be emphasised that this section does not provide an in-depth account of Gramsci's Marxism. Instead, what this section does is to consider two aspects of Gramsci's work which are important to this study. The first notion to be considered will be that of hegemony, although it will be argued that the hegemonic notion developed by Williams is a progressive modification of the initial term. The second notion to be considered will be that of a dialectical process between what Gramsci refers to as the organic and conjunctural aspects of crisis. This provides a major principle around which I shall focus the study of South African sport as a cultural form.

18

What distinguished Gramsci's work from that of Marx was the degree of importance attached to the area of politics in bringing about what Gramsci referred to as revolutionary consciousness. In Gramsci's conception, the only true revolutionary theory was one that went beyond all forms of economic determinism. While not denying the primacy of the mode of production in shaping historical development, Gramsci argued that, during periods of unrest,[4] i.e. conjunctural periods, super-structural elements, such as politics, must have primacy over the economic base.

> The claim presented as an essential postulate of historical materialism, that every fluctuation of politics and ideology can be presented and expounded as an immediate expression of the structure (i.e. base), must be contested in theory as primitive infantilism, and combated in practice with the authentic testimony of Marx (Gramsci, 1980: 407).

What did Gramsci mean by hegemony and why is it a relevant conception for helping to organise the issues at hand? In differentiating two fundamental types of political control, Gramsci emphasised direct physical coercion on the one hand and control through hegemony on the other. According to Gramsci's concept (1980: 39), hegemony meant:

> The permeation throughout civil society . . . of an entire system of values, beliefs, attitudes, morality, etc. that is in one way or another supportive of the established order and the class interests that dominate it.

Gramsci's notion of hegemony relied heavily on forms of ideological control. As such, hegemony and ideology functioned through cementing and unifying the existing social order. In other words, the ideological subordination of the working class by the dominant class enabled the dominant class to rule by consent. If a social transformation was to come about, Gramsci argued that a 'counter-hegemony' would have to break the ideological bond between the ruling class and various sectors of the general population.

All of this raises a problem when applied to the South African situation. Apartheid systematically exploits blacks, especially in so far as it virtually guarantees their perpetual proletarianisation. Yet it is direct physical coercion rather than ideology and culture which has long been the foundation upon which apartheid has been based. None the less, in the face of world opinion and internal crisis, there has been a greater need on the part of the South African state to engage in ideological work. As opportunities have opened up in certain areas for some blacks, the problem of hegemony becomes more critical.

As a general rule, hegemony works through ideology, but it does not always consist of false ideas, perceptions and definitions. It often works primarily by inserting members of the subordinate classes into key institutions and structures which support the power and social authority of the dominant order. Yet, these forms of mobility are often little more than simple incorporation. While society opens up for a few individuals, class power, expressed as the capacity to define economic and cultural standards, remains unchanged. This type of power is referred to by Lukes (1974: 23) as:

> The power to define the agenda, to shape
> preferences, to prevent conflict from arising in the
> first place or to contain conflict when it does arise by
> defining what sorts of resolution are reasonable or
> realistic within the existing order.

According to Gramsci, the major areas where hegemony was exercised were civil society and the state. One of the appealing parts of Gramsci's work on hegemony is that through considering all men as intellectuals there is at least some scope for addressing the part played by individual agents in the explanation of domination and subordination. For Gramsci, a hegemonic relationship was an educational or intellectual relationship. All people in society were seen as intellectuals but not all men in society had the opportunity to function as intellectuals.

While accepting Gramsci's view of intellectuals, it is important to realise that hegemony itself is rarely sustained by any one class or culture. The content of any hegemony is partially determined by those subcultures, counter-cultures and oppositional class fractions which form a hegemonic bloc. Hegemony or a hegemonic society is not simply class rule, it requires at least some degree of consent from the subordinate class which in turn has to be won and secured (Hall and Jefferson, 1976: 39). This struggle against class hegemony takes place within the very same civil society to which Gramsci referred. In short, what is being said is that, while the dominant culture retains power, its repertoire of control is continuously challenged in complex and subtle ways. As a result this repertoire of control is often weakened and transformed. Hegemony, as Williams (1977: 110) sees it, is always an active process.

Hegemony can never be taken for granted, but it has to be continually fought for afresh. This requires persistent activities to maintain and strengthen the social authority of the ruling class in all areas of civil society. This process can be seen at work most clearly in periods when the hegemony of the dominant culture is endangered. There may ensue a fairly prolonged period of instability and transition during which the system of alliances forming the basis for hegemonic rule has to undergo far-reaching changes and a process of restructuring in order to survive. It is precisely this process of restructuring which has led a number of writers[5] on South Africa to suggest that the current crisis facing South Africa is best conceptualised within the organic and conjunctural sense of the word crisis.

It is necessary here to elaborate further on Gramsci's distinction between organic and conjunctural crises. According to Gramsci (1980: 178):

> A crisis occurs sometimes lasting for decades. This exceptional duration means that incurable structural contradictions have revealed themselves (reached maturity), and that despite this, the political forces, which are struggling to conserve and defend the existing structure itself, are making every effort to cure them, within certain limits, and to overcome them. These incessant and persistent efforts ... form the terrain of the conjunctural and it is upon this terrain that the forces of opposition must organise.

As Boggs points out, Gramsci's model of revolutionary transformation departed significantly from Lenin's in terms of the national task of Marxism (Boggs, 1980: 114). It is not necessary, I believe, to differentiate in detail the differences between Lenin's[6] model and Gramsci's model of revolutionary transformation only to point out that at the core of these crucial differences for Gramsci was the dual perspective,

> rooted in the dichotomy between force and consent in politics, which he conceptualised in terms of 'organic' and conjunctural dimensions of change. (Boggs, 1980: 114)

It is crucial to realise that this dichotomy refers only to what Gramsci referred to as transformative moments in society. These transformative moments need not necessarily be short term in duration, but could last for decades. As noted earlier, by conjunctural, Gramsci meant the passing and momentary period of crisis in which the contesting political forces struggle for state power. The 'organic' aspect of political struggle on the other hand referred to the long-range contestation for ideological hegemony.

The term 'conjuncture', writes Simon (1982: 38), is similar to what Lenin used to call the current situation or the balance of political forces existing at the present moment to which political tactics have to be applied. What Gramsci stressed was that the current situation had not only to be understood in terms of economic and political problems but more importantly by the incessant and persistent efforts which are made to conserve and defend the existing system.

In the South African situation these 'incessant efforts' are clearly visible in terms of Botha's reform strategy which involves a restructuring of the class system and the introduction of a number of policies which have attempted to modify the rhetoric of apartheid. In the context of this study particular attention is given to South Africa's multinational sports policy; however, this alone does not constitute a conjunctural response which has to be seen in conjunction with other changes such as the politics of separate development.

The term 'organic' in the Gramscian sense refers to a deep crisis, a structural crisis which leads to a conjunctural response. The organic crisis with which Gramsci was centrally concerned was the crisis in Italy lasting from about 1910 to 1921 which was eventually resolved by the rise of Mussolini's fascism. During this period there began a profound upheaval in the structure of Italian society affecting all classes. This was marked (Gramsci, 1980: 52–120) by a rise in the militancy of the working class and of sections of the peasantry. The strength of the working class with its revolutionary tendencies ensured that the hegemony of the Northern Industrialists disintegrated. However, through lack of leadership the movement was unable to build an alliance capable of sustaining an effective challenge to the dominant culture.

One conclusion that Gramsci (1980: 222) draws from these considerations is that a dominant 'social form' always has marginal possibilities for further development and organisational improvement, and in particular can count on the relative weakness of the rival progressive force. It is necessary for the dominant social form to preserve this weakness; if it cannot, then transformation will take place.

It is possible to see South Africa as being in a state of organic crisis in the Gramscian sense. It is not necessary here to expand on this assertion in great detail since it shall be discussed at more length in Chapter 2. Briefly stated, the organic crisis in South Africa can be identified by: (1) structural contradictions which have characterised the accumulation process under racial capitalism; (2) the political struggle within the ruling National Party between the *verkramptes* and the *verligtes*; (3) the escalation of resistance from a number of liberation forces both internally and externally; and (4) the conjunctural response from the political ruling party.

As Hall points out, it is important that we get the organic and conjunctural aspects of any crisis into a proper relationship (Hall, 1981: 116). What defines the conjunctural, the immediate terrain of struggle, is not simply the given economic conditions, but precisely the incessant and persistent efforts which are being made to conserve and defend the status quo. If the crisis is deep, i.e. organic, then these efforts cannot merely be defensive, but are formative. They will be formative in the sense that a new balance of forces, and the emergence of new elements, philosophies, etc. will attempt to put together a new historical bloc. Hall (1981: 117) goes on to talk of:

> a profound restructuring of the state and ideological discourse which construct the crisis and represent it as it is lived as a practical reality, new programmes

and policies pointing to a new result, a new sort of
settlement within certain limits. These do not
emerge: they have to be constructed.

The relationship between the organic and the conjunctural
must be seen to be dialectical in that a reciprocal interaction
exists between the two. By this, I mean that the conjunctural
is not merely a response to the organic, but a reflection of the
crisis itself. Yet, while Gramsci referred to the primacy of the
party in moments of crisis, he also emphasised the importance
of totality. The totality consisted not only of the party, but of
a larger complex of social groups which made up the total
milieu. The totality function was to dismantle the conjunctural
in that it should be seen by all the oppositional forces to be
nothing more than a reflection of the organic crisis. Hence, in
reference to the conjunctural, Gramsci wrote, it is upon this
terrain that the forces of opposition must organise (Gramsci,
1980: 178).

The argument that has been made in this chapter is that
pluralist and idealist theories of race relations are inadequate
in helping to explain South Africa in the 1980s. As a contrast
I have suggested that historical materialism provides a better
understanding and meaning with regard to social-historical
analysis of South Africa as a state in crisis. My argument is
that it is entirely appropriate to see much of this as directly
applicable to the current situation in South Africa, in which
the 'modernising' of racial domination can be seen as conjunctural response to the growing contradictions which have historically evolved through the process of capital accumulation
under apartheid.

Chapter 2 concerns itself more specifically with the crisis
that has evolved in South Africa. It addresses questions such
as: 'What are the key dimensions of the organic crisis of South
Africa's racial capitalism?' 'What are the concrete strategies
which are being mounted by the dominant culture, in the context of the organic crisis, in order to defend the essential limits
of the present South African system?' However, before doing
so, it is necessary to specify the main components which, historically, have come to shape the racialist capitalist system itself and to identify those actors and formations who play the
most important contemporary roles in bringing about change.

TWO

A HERITAGE
OF STRUGGLE

Having developed a general theoretical point of departure in
Chapter 1, I now want to consider the crisis which has evolved
in South Africa. More specifically it might be stated that this
chapter looks at the following themes. Firstly, the process of
capital accumulation which outlines historically the importance
of such factors as the 'native reserves', conflicting interests of
British and Dutch capital and the development of capitalism
under apartheid since its inception in 1948. The historical perspective must not give rise to the idea that such a formation
emerged without a struggle. In many ways South African history is a heritage of struggle between not only oppressed cultures and a dominant minority white culture, but also between
various ruling factions within this dominant minority.
Secondly, it is argued that only through the development of
consciousness can the economic crisis, which faced South
Africa in the late 1970s, be transformed into organic crisis. It
is only after the 'Soweto' uprisings of 1976 that the black
working class, in particular the labour movement, has mounted
a major challenge to the dominant white minority. The significance of the 1976–7 rebellion lies not in the fact that it was
crushed in part through military repression, but that it advanced once more the development of black working-class consciousness. Finally, this chapter outlines the conjunctural response to the crisis in the light of the present government's
policy of 'rationalising apartheid', since 1979, under Prime
Minister P.W. Botha.

The heritage of struggle

for all the overt signs of race as the mechanism of
domination, the legal and institutional domination of
the white minority over the black majority has its
orgins in and is perpetuated by, economic
exploitation (Slovo, 1976: 18).

This economic exploitation has rested upon dependent
wage-labour relations in which, in order to survive, Africans
in particular have had to sell their labour at relatively little or
no expense to the state. Since 1652 when the first European
colony settled on the Cape, two fundamental features have
maintained coherence throughout pre-capitalist and capitalist
social formations in the Republic of South Africa. Firstly,
through slavery, the formation of native reserves in the nine-
teenth century and through establishing a Bantustan strategy
in the twentieth century, there has always been a continuous
supply of cheap black labour in South Africa. Although the
mode of production may have changed, the supply of black
labour has been continuous. Secondly, although various dominant cultures have evolved since 1652, they can all be characterised as a white, European ruling class. The struggle for
hegemonic rule has predominantly involved conflict between
British and Afrikaner capitalist interests and black resistance
to forms of domination.

Since 1652, when the Dutch East India Company formed a
settlement on the Cape, two centuries of pre-capitalist forms
of exploitation such as slavery and feudal relations of production by which white settler farmers extracted rent in cash or
labour services from African peasantry have evolved. It is at
this same period in time that the heritage of African struggle
against forms of white domination also developed. Jan van
Riebeeck, the leader of the first party of colonists, wrote:

the prisoners . . . having been asked the reason why
they had caused us this trouble, declare for no other
reason than that they saw that we kept in possession
the best lands . . . and that everywhere . . . we
endeavored to establish ourselves so permanently as if
we intended never to leave again. (from Rogers, 1980:
5)

26

With the abolition of slavery in the British Empire in 1834, both British and Dutch farming interests demanded that new sources of labour had to be found and stabilised. The problem in part was answered through the creation of native reserves in which Africans, confined to reserved areas of land, were used whenever necessary to support the white economy through being forced to enter into strictly controlled labour relations. Although the development of 'native reserves' and their modern equivalent, which, under the rhetoric of apartheid, have been labelled 'Bantustans' or 'tribal homelands', have existed since 1841, it is far too simplistic, I believe, to consider the reserves solely as labour pools for the facilitation of capital accumulation. That the reserves provide such a function is not denied. Yet, it is crucial to point out that certain forms of pre-capitalist means of production existed within the reserves. For instance, during the period of segregation[1] agriculture provided Africans with some limited income. Furthermore the ancient tribal system of authority, which still exists today, provided an internal mechanism of control. It is precisely these complex relations of production internally and externally which have enabled the process of capital accumulation in South Africa to continue during the twentieth century.

In *One Azania, One Nation*, No Sizwe[2] (1979: 35) makes a number of crucial points. Firstly,

> the reserves served to produce not proletarians
> according to the classical definition, but rather
> workers who retained access to albeit limited means
> of production and who also had to sell their labour
> power for at least part of the time in order to survive.

What is being argued here is that the maintenance of pre-capitalist relations in the 'reserves' affected the value of the migrant workers' labour power. The wage subsidy provided through a communal mode of production in the reserves helped to suppress the value of the Africans' labour power which meant that cheap labour was provided by the African at little or no expense to the wages bill of capital. This analysis is reiterated by Magubane (1979: 95) when he says that:

> The reserves offered cheap, hardened manual

labourers eminently exploitable and with the
expenses of their reproduction charged elsewhere.

Furthermore, from the point of view of the urban industrial
worker, the standards of living in the 'reserves' symbolised the
physical minimum of human survival. By thus helping to
freeze and entrench historically the accepted minimum for survival, the reserves ensured that the wages bill of capital remained relatively static and even a declining percentage of the
Gross National Product.

Secondly, No Sizwe argues, in industrial capitalist economies, such as Britain, a certain percentage of the work force is
normally kept unemployed (Marx's 'reserve army of labour').
This reserve army, through competition for jobs, holds down
the level of wages and, at the same time, helps to discipline the
employed labour force which at least theoretically can be replaced by the unemployed. Since the unemployed must eat
and live to be able to survive for these functions, their existence
is catered to by the state through unemployment benefits, etc.
However, in South Africa this is not the case since:

> the burden of supporting the bulk of the labour
> reserve army has fallen predominantly on the
> reserves. It is the reserves that have made possible
> the maintenance of these workers . . . at minimal cost
> to the State . . . but at the expense of the workers and
> the peasants themselves (Sizwe, 1979: 36).

The extent to which various cultural groupings have been
oppressed historically, in South Africa, must not give rise to
the idea that this oppression was accepted without a struggle
by the African and other oppressed workers. Severe and in-
tense struggles were waged throughout history and are still
being waged by the exploited labouring mass of people in
South Africa. Although specific instances will be referred to
throughout this study, at this point it suffices to offer a brief
historical synopsis of the struggle which has evolved and is
facing South Africa today.

As South African capitalism developed, blacks formed
numerous political, cultural and trade union groups to try and
advance their struggles for class and national emancipation.

Scarcely a decade went by without major battles being fought: the first mass black demonstrations and strikes in the 1910s, the meteoric growth in African unionisation in the 1920s, attempts at forging broad African unity in the 1930s, work stoppages, urban risings and mass protest campaigns of the 1940s, boycotts, general strikes and massive civil disobedience actions of the 1950s, widespread rebellion following the Sharpeville massacre in the 1960s, labour unrest and student rebellions of the 1970s, and finally, bombings and labour tension during the early part of the 1980s. Throughout this struggle, black working-class culture played a central role. Even when workers were not involved with the leadership of various political campaigns, their class interests left a strong imprint on the demands raised and the forms of struggle undertaken. (See Appendix 1.)

The development of capitalism during the twentieth century, in both British mining and Dutch agricultural interests, rested upon labour repression and supply. In *South Africa after Zimbabwe*, Callinicos (1981) makes the point that it was upon the marriage of maize and gold, an alliance of mining and agricultural capital, that the Union of South Africa was founded in 1910 (Callinicos, 1981: 74). It was only after 1910 that a co-ordinated British/Afrikaner offensive against the African landowners was possible. The offensive took the form of the 1913 and 1936 Native Land Acts which reduced the amount of land allocated to the reserves to 13 per cent of the total land.[3] Up until 1913 the reserves had been maintained by either British or Dutch Afrikaner interests; the co-ordinated offensive formalised the reserve system and chartered the course of 'native' policy for the rest of the twentieth century. The consequences of the 1913 Act in particular were not fully realised until the 1930s and 1940s. However, these related developments can only be understood in relation to major changes that occurred within the overall structure of industrial capitalism in the case of South Africa.

Firstly, as Luckhardt and Wall point out (1980: 47), the rapid process of industrialisation during the mid-1920s resulted in the manufacturing sector contributing a greater proportion to the National Income than the agricultural sector for the first time in 1930. By 1943 manufacturing had outstripped mining. However, industrialisation also led to the formation of

29

an urban proletariat, both white and black. Poor white Afrikaners entered the cities at an estimated rate of 11,000[4] per year
between 1921 and 1936. The African proletariat increased by
even greater proportions. The urban African population treb-
led between 1921 and 1946. Secondly, the traditional categories
of skilled and unskilled labour rapidly gave way to a new kind
of worker, what Luckhardt and Wall refer to as the semi-
skilled operative, a human appendage to the machine (Luckhardt and Wall, 1980: 48). Both Africans and Afrikaners (especially women) assumed these positions as they entered the
urban work force.

This proletarianisation of the black people, together with a
number of other factors such as overcrowding in the reserves
and rapid industrialisation, found expression in a range of mass
struggles which characterised the mid- and late 1930s and the
1940s. The neglect of the reserves and the overcrowding
created by the Native Land Act led to the situation where the
wage subsidy function of the reserves disappeared and consequently eroded the basis of a cheap black labour supply. The
scale of the challenge to the system represented by the black
working class was brought home in 1946, when the African
Mine Workers' Union called a strike around demands which
amounted effectively to the destruction of the migrant labour
system. The significance of the strike cannot be overemphas-
ised. It marks a dominant moment in South African history on
two accounts: firstly, it still remains the largest single strike in
South African history, and secondly, it was a strike that was
violently crushed by the state. As O'Meara (1975: 46) points
out:

> Occasionally . . . one event seems to crystallise the
> contradictions and conflicts of an entire stage of
> social development and the reactions to it point the
> way to the future development of a particular social
> formation. Despite its apparent failure, the 1946
> African Miners' strike was such a milestone in South
> Africa's social and political development.

In short, the strike symbolised the struggle of the Africans
against class exploitation and oppression. The largest strike in
South African history (in terms of participants) signalled the

end of one era and the beginning of another, namely apartheid rule after 1948.

However, the whole question of mass struggle by the oppressed classes must be 'seen in conjunction with the contradictions and tensions which existed among the various fractions of the ruling class during the period immediately prior to 1948. The central question was the response of the state to the continuing influx of black labour. While the reserve and migrant labour system has in the past benefited the mining and agricultural industries, it had to a certain extent undermined the growing secondary and tertiary industries. White wage earners felt threatened by any policy of black trade union recognition or any policy which meant permanent status for blacks in urban areas. Small industrial capitalists felt that their competitive position would be threatened by the significant increases in black wages that the United Party policy seemed to entail. The answer, writes No Sizwe, to this contradiction between the different fractions of the ruling class was the National Party's policy of apartheid (Sizwe, 1979: 42).

The 1950s were a period of low and uncertain growth, a situation that in part reflected the doubts of foreign capitalists about apartheid strategy. The most obvious development during this period was the much greater prominence of 'Afrikaans-speaking' capital which formed the power base of the National Party. In *Crisis in South Africa*, Saul and Gelb (1981: 18) write of this period:

> The burgeoning state sector provided the groups clustered around the Nationalist Party with economic clout to direct the path of accumulation in their own interests, as distinct from the interests of foreign and local English capital.

A number of corporations[5] developed through the awarding of an increasing number of state contracts, particularly in mining, industry and commerce. After the Sharpeville riots of 1960, in which sixty-seven demonstrators died and more than 180 were injured, it became clear that the apartheid regime was, for the meantime, capable of crushing black resistance. Once stability was obtained, foreign capital power poured into South Africa attracted by low wages and high profits. During the 1950s

31

South Africa became a prime target for international capital when the latter sought markets for high technology and capital intensive commodities. In particular, foreign investment began to pour into the manufacturing industry. By the mid-1960s direct investment in the manufacturing industry was the predominant form of foreign participation in the South African economy, although this was closely followed by American investment in mining. (Multinationals such as Amax, Newmont, Inco and Falconbridge all developed new mines in South Africa during the 1960s.)

The role of foreign firms is summarised by Harsch (1980) in *South Africa: White Rule, Black Revolt*. The argument is essentially that despite occasional criticism of apartheid, the basic approach of imperialist powers such as America, Britain, Germany and Japan (South Africa's major investors) is to help the South African regime survive. South African stability plays a major role in terms of economic investment. For instance, 'Washington', writes Harsch, 'does not favour any major advances by the black liberation movement' (Harsch, 1980: 113). Consequently level of investment is dependent on level of stability.

South Africa, on the other hand, was eager to attract foreign investment for a number of reasons. Firstly, to build up certain key sectors of the economy. For instance, by the early 1970s, General Motors, Ford and Chrysler controlled the majority of the South African auto market. Secondly, foreign economic investment gave South African firms access to advanced technology. For instance, Saul and Gelb point out that the boom period of the 1960s was sustained by sophisticated technology in a number of manufacturing interests such as computers, synthetics, engineering and chemicals (Saul and Gelb, 1981: 20). Finally, South African authorities have been able to take advantage of the prominent involvement by foreign firms for political purposes. Pointing to the support and solidarity of their allies in Europe, America and Japan, etc., the authorities have sought to foster an image of stability and strength to convince resistance groups that Pretoria's foreign backers would not allow their vital stake in South Africa to be threatened by an overthrow of white minority rule.

While the 1960s and early 1970s marked a boom period for apartheid in terms of development, the period from 1973 until

1980 earmarked the beginning of a crisis period from which South Africa has not yet fully recovered. The extent of the crisis can be illustrated by several different indices provided by Saul and Gelb (1981: 20). The real growth rate, which averaged 5.7 per cent annually in the late 1960s, was negative in the first half of 1976 and zero in 1977. Balance of payments difficulties resulting from state expenditures on defence and investment projects were compounded by the fall in the price of gold during 1975. Furthermore, during 1976–7 a drop in foreign investment occurred as a direct result of the unstable position in South Africa after the start of the Soweto events.

The economic crisis served to pinpoint some of the inherent weaknesses of the apartheid regime. Firstly, the logic of South Africa's capitalist economy, like those of the foreign investors, demands that it expands its markets. Yet the home market has been restricted in part by the limited purchasing power of the African market as a result of low wages. Furthermore, as a result of political changes in the other African states, such as Zimbabwe, Angola and Mozambique, South Africa's national markets in the rest of Africa have been slowly eroded. Secondly, high levels of mechanisation in mining, manufacturing and agriculture led to high levels of unemployment. As both Callinicos (1981) and Saul and Gelb (1981) indicate, black unemployment in May 1978 equalled 20 per cent of the economically active population and the number of white, coloured and Asian unemployed increased by 250 per cent between 1974–7. Finally, despite high levels of unemployment the influx of non-white workers into areas of employment previously reserved for whites only increased the degree of dependence upon black labour. Not only do non-whites provide a cheap labour supply, but they now also provide an increasing number of skilled workers. This transformation has served to increase the bargaining power of a certain class of non-white worker.

The economic crisis facing South Africa was in part averted during the early 1980s by a gold boom. As Callinicos (1981: 117) explains:

> The continued shift of OPEC funds into gold pushed
> the price sharply upwards and forced the US
> Treasury to admit defeat and abandon its sales of
> gold. Panic caused by the Soviet occupation of

33

Afghanistan led to peak gold prices of $835 an ounce during 1980.

This was in comparison to $225 an ounce in November 1979. The rising gold price implied a radical improvement in South Africa's economic prospects. The soaring gold price made it easier for South Africa to borrow abroad. By February 1980 the *Financial Mail* was reporting a 'capital spending spree' in both public and private sectors. However, the rise in gold prices proved to be only a temporary respite for the regime. As Saul and Gelb point out (1981: 24), inflation, which consistently stood at 10 per cent after 1974, rose to 14 per cent in 1980 and close to 20 per cent at the beginning of 1981. They go on to argue that:

> Even although larger gold revenues may buy some relief from technological dependence ... they cannot, in the light of South Africa's position within the world economy, imply a permanent balance of payments surplus. Thus in the last quarter of 1980, a combination of rising imports due to the boom and a dip in the gold price had already moved the current account back into deficit. (Saul and Gelb; 1981: 25)

However, far more serious than the economic crisis facing South Africa during the 1980s is the threat posed by the increasing development of black consciousness. The bombings of the Sasol oil plants during June 1980 made clear for the third time in less than a decade that large-scale population struggles have erupted inside South Africa. It is the development of consciousness among Africans during the 1970s and 1980s that I now want to address.

The development of black consciousness

Despite continuous attempts by the South African ruling class to suppress and contain the forward movement of the African working class, history has demonstrated the futility of their tactics. (Luckhardt and Wall, 1980: 273)

The relative political quiescence during the boom from 1960 to 1970 did not last long. Ironically, black political activity during the 1970s was bolstered by the same economic expansion upon which the dominant white culture thrived. The growth of the urbanised black working class provided a solid foundation for the emergence of new forms of struggle. In particular, the heritage of struggle during the 1970s centred around student organisations and mass strike actions by workers.

The South African Students' Organisation (SASO) under the leadership of Steve Biko sought during the early 1970s to draw a sharp line between oppressors and the oppressed. Biko explained in *I Write What I Like*:

> The biggest mistake the black world ever made was
> to assume that whoever opposed apartheid was an
> ally. For a long time the black world has been
> looking only at the governing party and not so much
> at the whole power structure as the object of their
> rage. In a sense the very political vocabulary that the
> blacks have used has been inherited from the liberals.
> (Biko, 1978: 63–4).

In early 1972, SASO action centred around the expulsion of Ramothibi Tiro, the Student Union President who had urged black graduates to become politically active. On expulsion, students of Tiro's university boycotted all lectures. Solidarity actions quickly spread to other campuses and, significantly, white students at a number of English-speaking campuses staged a series of protests in solidarity with black students. Eventually black and white revolts were crushed by police and security forces. However, as Harsch points out (1980: 262), more important than any concrete success or failure was the impact upon the political consciousness of young blacks. For the first time in more than a decade students had openly demonstrated against state policies.

During January and February of 1973 strikes in the Durban area spread from one factory to another. In most cases the strikes resulted in wage gains of between 15–20 per cent. However, again, as in the case of the 1972 student action, the impact of the strikes was more profound. From the perspective of the working class the wage gains were important but the primary legacy of this round of strikes was an alteration in the consciousness of both black and white workers, and a new sense of their own power and of their ability to challenge capital successfully. As the Standard Bank Review said in April 1973:

> The days are past when employers could bargain
> with Bantu workers from a position of unchallenged
> strength.

This new power was in part reflected by the revival of black trade union organisation among the black working class. As Callinicos points out (1981: 121), white, coloured and Asian workers of the Trade Union Council of South Africa (TUCSA) began to set up parallel unions for African workers. However, much more important was the independent black workers' movement which consisted of three main groups, the Federation of South African Trade Unions (FOSATU), the Western Province General Workers' Union (WPGWU) and the Food and Canning Workers' Union (FCWU). These three in particular showed a firm commitment to union democracy, control by membership and shop floor organisation. Yet, as Saul and Gelb point out (1981: 168), although class consciousness and struggle had been sharpened as a result of the 1972 and 1973 militant actions the political challenge to the dominant classes was, as yet, not adequate to transform economic crisis into organic crisis. The advance of this kind was the major achievement of the 1976-7 rebellion which spread across the country but which is labelled according to its point of origin 'the Soweto Riots'.

The sixteen-month period which began on 16 June 1976 with the demonstration by Soweto High School Students against the use of Afrikaans in their schools was extremely important.[6] The initial concern to eliminate Afrikaans as a medium of instruction in schools soon grew into a demand to scrap the entire Bantu Education system and ultimately to destroy apartheid itself. Involving other militant groups, the Soweto Students' Representative Council (SSRC) was supported by mass strike action by a number of black workers in major cities such as Johannesburg and Cape Town who, acting upon advice given by the African National Congress (ANC),

stayed away from work. The Cape Town action was particularly significant in that it represented a unified front between
African, coloured and Asian workers. The challenge to the
state by 'Soweto' is perhaps symbolised in the words of SSRC
President Khotso Seathoo (from Harsch, 1980: 297), and consequently is worth quoting at length:

> We shall rise up and destroy a political ideology that
> is designed to keep us in a perpetual state of
> oppression and subserviency. We shall oppose the
> economic system that is keeping us in a non-ending
> state of poverty. We shall not stand a social system of
> discrimination that has become an insult to our
> human dignity. We shall reject the whole system of
> Bantu Education whose aim is to reduce us, mentally
> and physically, into 'hewers of wood and drawers of
> water' for the white racist masters. Our whole 'being'
> rebels against the whole South African system of
> existence, the system of apartheid that is killing us
> psychologically and physically.

The revolt wound down in early 1978 in large part as a
response to several factors: the wholesale repression which had
caused 700 deaths between June 1976 and October 1977; ex-
haustion on the part of the movement; and to a lack of leadership and general co-ordination. However, the significance here
is not in the eventual failure of 'Soweto', but the further development of black working-class consciousness which, by this
stage, had transformed the initial economic crisis into an
organic crisis. The 'Soweto' uprisings, write Saul and Gelb
(1981: 110):

> substantially reinforced the legacy of the Durban
> strikes, their mental sediment: the intellectual,
> cultural growth of the proletariat.

A cooling-off period at the end of 1978 after Soweto proved
to be only a temporary respite for the regime. The first signs
of renewed struggle came in May 1979 when a national con-
sumer boycott developed in response to a strike by African and
coloured workers at Fatti's and Moni's pasta factory in Cape

Town. This was only the beginning of a wave of militancy which carried South Africa into the 1980s. Again, Saul and Gelb point out (1981: 111) that during the first six months of 1980 the number of strikes was double that of the entire previous year. For instance, by the end of April 1980, 100,000 students were estimated to be involved in school boycotts all over the Western Cape. According to Callinicos (1981: 133) several things should be noted about the boycott. Firstly, there was a high degree of discipline and organisation displayed by the boycotters, somewhat in contrast to the rather chaotic beginnings of the 1976 uprisings. Secondly, the level of political consciousness was higher than in 1976. Finally, although the core of the boycott was in the African and coloured community, it soon spread to other oppressed groups such as the Asian community.

Furthermore, the ANC bomb attack on the Sasol oil plants in June 1980 represented a significant departure from past strategies. As Barrell says (1980: 524), South Africa had never before witnessed so sophisticated and costly an act of sabotage. Although attacks on only two of the four targets succeeded, the operation revealed the presence of formidable, well-trained forces. During 1981 some 170 strikes by black workers were carried out. FOSATU notes in the 1981 report that of some ninety strikes in FOSATU organised factories, fifty-three were won (Bermen, 1982). The present challenge has been strengthened by the fact that the coloureds, the occupants of the dangerous no-man's-land between whites and Africans, and viewed by some as brown Afrikaners, now appear to have aligned themselves firmly with the majority African population against the dominant white minority.

The chief purpose of this chapter so far has been to trace the evolution of the crisis in South Africa from a simple economic to an organic crisis. The presence of such an organic crisis, as already mentioned, is only further underlined by the efforts of the state to conserve and defend the existing structure. The conjunctural response to this crisis does not merely emerge 'naturally' but is constructed actively by the dominant culture. The final part of this chapter considers one such response in the terms of Prime Minister P.W. Botha's strategy aimed at rationalising apartheid.

The conjunctural response to the crisis

Although pressure from foreign investors and sectors of the ruling class for major reforms within the existing system had been in evidence for some time, it was only after 'Soweto' that major changes in South African policy were actually implemented. Immediately after 'Soweto', the then Prime Minister, Vorster, initiated a few minor changes such as scrapping compulsory use of Afrikaans as the main language medium in African schools. However, it was only after Vorster resigned and P.W. Botha became Prime Minister in September 1978 that South Africa stepped up what many foreign investors have considered to be concessions to the black majority population.

The message which gave Prime Minister Botha electoral success was simply 'adapt or die'. (The reason for this statement has already been explained in this chapter in the light of the organic crisis facing South Africa.) As the new Prime Minister pointed out:

> If South Africa is to enter into an era of relative
> stability and prosperity, government must ensure that
> as many people as possible share in that prosperity.
> ... Defusing the social time-bomb can only be
> achieved through negotiation with the authentic
> leaders of the black people. (from Saul and Gelb,
> 1981: 2)

Both Botha and Foreign Minister Koornhof consciously tried to present their new measures as proof of the regime's willingness to modify and cater for black aspirations. For instance, Harsch (1980: 174) notes how figures were released to show that expenditure on black education, housing and other services had all increased since 1979. It will suffice in this chapter only to point out the core of this 'modernising apartheid strategy' since the major point being made is that the existence of such a 'conjunctural response' only serves further to underline the crisis facing South Africa in the 1980s.

Apart from South Africa's new sporting policy, which is examined in the next chapter, the main thrust of Botha's strategy has revolved around the establishment of a black middle class through the Riekert and Wiehahn proposals. The effect of these proposals has been to increase the degree of dependency which both the independent Bantustans and neighbouring African states have upon the South African economy. Together these proposals were aimed at diffusing the black liberation struggle in southern Africa while at the same time superficially presenting an image of change to the outside.

The Riekert Report published in May 1979 attempted to defuse the extent of black militancy by developing a black middle class. Under Section Ten of the Urban Areas Act, no African can remain inside an Urban Area for longer than seventy-two hours. Those exempt from this rule, the skilled Africans, are generally referred to as Section Ten dwellers. It was these Section Tenners who, so the Riekert Report recommended, were to form the basis of a new black middle class by being provided with substantial advantages in the labour market such as approved housing and the right to have their family with them. Those without Section Ten rights, however, were to remain in the Bantustans and experience a tightening-up of the pass laws and influx control. Thus, the Bantustans still continued to perform their functions as a labour reserve and a dumping ground for the non-productive black populations.

To summarise, the Riekert Report provided the machinery whereby, firstly, African resistance was reduced through developing a black middle class and through a stricter control over those Africans who did not qualify for middle-class status; secondly, the problem of the lack of skilled labour was in part solved by allowing Africans to take up skilled jobs, and, finally, the Report indicated to foreign investors that change, albeit small, was taking place in South Africa.

The suggestions made by the Riekert Report complemented those made earlier by the Wiehahn Commission which recommended that:

> Africans should be permitted to form trade unions
> registered under the Industrial Conciliation Act
> which makes strikes effectively illegal. (Callinicos,
> 1981: 205)

Luckhardt and Wall (1980: 459) note, however, that while the propagandists of apartheid have spent millions in promoting this as an end to racial discrimination in the industrial relations field the facts of the matter speak otherwise. The purpose of encouraging the registration of presently unregistered trade unions lies not so much in promoting equality but in identifying sections of the black militant majority so that they can be controlled under a repressive industrial relations system first introduced in 1924. Thus, by incorporating the African workers' unions, the government hopes to eliminate their independence and reduce their militancy. As SACTU stated in its condemnation of the Wiehahn Commission at the ILO Conference in June 1979:

> SACTU has always maintained that recognition must come through the struggle and strength of the workers vis-à-vis the exploiters – it can never be a concession granted by the oppressors themselves. Legality must not be confused with emancipation (from Luckhardt and Wall, 1980: 460)

While both the Wiehahn and Riekert Commissions have suggested to the outside world that South African policies were changing with regard to increased recognition of its black majority, in reality both Commissions intensified state control over the African worker. Both Commissions presuppose the entire apartheid system and only attempt to make that system of repression and exploitation more efficient. Both bodies were set up by the apartheid regime, and staffed and implemented by its own supporters to deal with its own crisis. Every single piece of industrial relations legislation introduced in South Africa since 1924 had attempted to restrict the freedom of the South African working class. These recent examples are no different in that they serve only to reinforce the lessons learned from history.

Attempts to increase South African hegemony over the whole of southern Africa (i.e. South Africa plus neighbouring African states) were further revealed as a result of Botha's plan unveiled in March 1979 and now named 'A Constellation of States in Southern Africa'. The major points were outlined by Plant (1982: 12) as:

41

- co-ordination to promote direct economic
  relationships between business sectors of the region
- technical and financial co-operation
- the promotion of investment
- the co-ordination of wage and salary policies to
  avoid a brain drain from the peripheral areas
- the co-ordination of economic and physical
  planning in terms of functional regions that often
  transcend international boundaries.

Although the grandest schemes were designed for South Africa's homelands, such as Transkei, Bophuthatswana, Ciskei, etc., the scheme was also aimed at increasing a dependence of African states such as Malawi and Zaire on the South African economy. The dependence of the states of southern Africa on the economic power of South Africa is a dominating feature of the political and economic position of many of the different states in the region. The situation is explained by Plant (1982: 25):

> Countries are different in their degree and type of
> dependence on South Africa. In Botswana, Lesotho,
> Namibia and Swaziland ... economic dependency
> manifests itself in the form of overwhelming
> economic dependence and political leverage by South
> Africa.
>
> Somewhat more loosely connected ... are Malawi,
> Mozambique, Zambia and Zimbabwe. Their
> economies are in some important respects linked to
> the centre but hardly to the extent of making them
> economic appendages.

The point that is being made here is that Botha's 'Constellation of States in Southern Africa' plan in reality serves to control even further those states which in the past have entered into economically dependent relations with South Africa. However, as already mentioned, such steps as underlined here must be viewed as a response to the crisis facing South Africa. The importance to Africans is not that such a response serves to control the masses even further but that, firstly, it has been through black militant action that such changes have resulted, and secondly, this 'new deal" is seen for what it really is, an attempt by the ruling class to diversify resistance, develop an incorporative economic strategy, and maintain white supreme power at all costs.

It is in the context of such 'reforms' that South Africa's sporting policies are considered in the next chapter. Very few areas have been more widely publicised by the white government than its multinational sports programme, first introduced in the early 1970s but only widely publicised since Botha came to power. Since 1978 Botha has continually insisted that a real effort would be made to make things inside the country seem better. The most visible areas of South African life were to be improved and to this end some of the peripheral edges of apartheid could be eroded. In the area of cultural life, the peripheral edges chosen were sport and recreation. Yet, like other aspects of the conjunctural, South Africa's multinational sports policy must be seen for what it really is.

THREE

THE POLITICAL ECONOMY OF WHITE SPORTING PRACTICE

In terms of influencing social change in South Africa, the area of sport seems relatively insignificant in that, even if sport was practised on a truly multiracial basis, it would have little effect on the well-being of the non-white majority who would still be confined to the compounds, townships and Bantustans after the game.[1] This point is made forcibly by Archer and Bouillon (1982: 303) when they say:

> All but the most fanatical sportsmen would probably
> agree that sport is not central to South African
> politics, or the liberation of the country from
> apartheid.

Yet, to understand the special political significance that can be attached to sport, it is essential to realise that the 'sports issue' is clearly bound up with the more fundamental issues which surround the policy of apartheid. Sport is extremely important politically because of the way that sport is used by the state in determining and influencing opinion towards South Africa. The white minority place so much emphasis on sport in their endeavours to portray an image of change to the outside world, that the struggle over sport cannot be ignored by social and political theorists.

44

This chapter focuses upon the way in which sport can be viewed as part of the conjunctural response to the growing crisis described in the last chapter. I shall argue that the emergence of a multinational sports policy in 1976 can be seen as one of the new programmes or policies constructed by the dominant culture in an attempt to conserve and maintain the status quo. More specifically, this chapter addresses the following themes: (1) the emergence of white sports[2] in South Africa; (2) the organisational structure of sport in South Africa (one of the direct consequences of a multinational sports policy has been the emergence of non-racial sporting organisations as a major form of resistance to the ideology of multiracial sport); (3) the emergence of South Africa's multinational sports policy; and (4) a critique of South African sporting reforms in terms of a discussion of a number of broader political and economic issues surrounding sport in South Africa.

The historical context

Very little historical material exists concerning the development of indigenous sporting forms in pre-colonial South Africa. The struggles and conflicts surrounding sporting cultural forms primarily revolve around those sporting forms which are important to the dominant white culture. Indigenous sporting forms of various types did however exist in pre-colonial South Africa. To prove and harden warriors the Zulus apparently organised orienteering, javelin-throwing and dance.[3] A wrestling tradition also existed from village to village with the winner declaring the subsequent feast open and the loser providing the banquet. These original sporting practices were gradually eroded as a direct result of colonialisation. Yet it is important to emphasise that traditional sporting practices did not simply die out but were marginalised and eventually replaced by white sporting practices. This abrupt change in the process of sporting evolution in South Africa started from the moment when the first settlers landed on the Cape in 1652. White settlers started to replace what they saw as primitive tribal sporting practices by white, 'civilising', European sports.

Early settler games revolved around the horse which played a crucial part in the Boer working life. Hunting and especially shooting were predominant recreational activities of this time. Although the first horse-racing club was not formed until 1802 regular horse races between British and Dutch settlers took place between 1795–1802. From its early beginnings in the Cape horse-racing quickly spread to Kimberley and Johannesburg until the South African Jockey Club was formed in 1882.

During the most active period of imperial expansion,[4] in which African peasants were forced to form wage-labour relations outside the reserves, a number of major sporting forms were introduced by the British Army and early British settlers. The first cricket match between settlers and natives took place in 1854, the first rugby club was established in 1876, while the formation of the all-white South African rugby board (SARB) took place in 1889.

These white European sports played a significant role in determining hierarchical sporting relations, not only between white and non-white cultures but also between British and Boer settlers. The social significance of cricket, for instance, is emphasised by Archer and Bouillon (1982, 88):

> Until the end of the 19th century, cricket had been a social game played popularly by all groups including Africans and Coloureds. The transformation into an imperial sport for the elite, conscious of its civilising, integrating mission in the world ... sharply reduced the game's audience amongst the blacks, the majority of whom were excluded from playing by material costs.

The relationship between cultures has always been a significant element in the emergence of white South African sport with sport itself being seen as one of the most typical expressions of leisure and rank during this period of imperialism. Consequently, sport became one of the major dividing lines between cultural groups and more specifically, one of the major symbols of white status.[5]

By the time the second Anglo–Boer war ended in 1902 a number of further sporting forms had been introduced. The first football club was formed in 1879; tennis, cycling, athletics, swimming and gymnastics had already been well established by 1889; the first British cricket tour took place in 1889 while the first rugby match played between the two armies took place on 29 April 1902. As Caffrey indicates (1973: 89):

> On April 28th 1902, one S.G. Maritz addressed a letter to the Honorable Major Edwards suggesting a rugby match.

During the period of Afrikaner nationalism and industrialisation between 1910 and 1948 the game of rugby symbolised the Afrikaner way of life. The mythical qualities surrounding rugby were closely linked to valued elements of Afrikaner culture such as religion, rugged frontier life-style and co-operation (Woods, 1981). Today, rugby is still seen as one of the strongholds of apartheid sport and of the South African ruling whites. Consequently, it has been one of the main target areas for resistance groups.[6] By the end of this period in history, rugby had already acquired much of its modern ethos within the white population. Symbolically, it already expressed the superiority of one culture over another in terms of the social relationships between dominant and subordinate cultures.

The institutionalisation of white sport in school physical education programmes during this period served as a further mechanism of social differentiation[7] between whites and non-whites. By 1939 physical education had been a compulsory subject in school and university programmes. However, the black population was hardly affected because only a small minority of the black children of school age were enrolled in school programmes. The introduction of physical recreation was only one aspect of sports development during the inter-war years. Expansion of the South African economy not only resulted in higher living standards for whites but also the creation of a number of new sporting federations.[8] In particular, the white sports boom was prominent in those industrial growth areas where increased industrial production resulted in further exploitation of cheap black labour ... labour which financed the installation of leisure and sporting facilities for the exclusively white work force (Archer and Bouillon, 1982: 36).

By the time the National Party came to power in 1948 and the apartheid policy emerged, a degree of segregation and inequality of opportunity between white and non-white athletes had evolved already in South African sport. There was little need, therefore, to impose a policy of apartheid upon specific sporting relations since social differentiation already existed. Furthermore, the general laws of apartheid rule rendered multi-racial sport impossible in that it was illegal for black and white athletes to mix openly in competition, as it was for black and white people to mix socially in society.

The period after 1948 has been marked by an increased intensity of struggle and conflict between competing sporting cultures in South Africa. It is not necessary at this stage to elaborate upon South Africa's tripartite sporting structure, merely to say that the struggle for sporting hegemony revolves around white, non-white and non-racial sporting forms in South Africa. It is this struggle for sporting hegemony with which this study is concerned.

By 1956 resistance to white sport had emerged as a result of exclusive recognition of the Non-Racial Table Tennis Board by the international table tennis federations and the demand for international recognition made by a number of black sporting federations. This form of cultural resistance led to the announcement made by the Minister of the Interior, Dr Donges, of South Africa's first official sports policy in 1956. This intervention incorporated formally the area of sport and the issue of non-racial sport for the first time into the political domain of the state. Sporting problems could no longer be resolved through purely sporting or non-political channels.

The initial transition of the black sporting federations towards non-racialism occurred between 1959 and 1962. Resistance to white sport centred around two non-racial sporting organisations, firstly, the South African Sports Association (SASA), and secondly the South African Non-Racial Olympic Committee (SAN-ROC) which was formed in 1962. However, while a number of black federations made the transition, a significant number became affiliated with white sporting federations (although they had dependent status).

From exile in London SAN-ROC organised its first major successful international campaign which culminated in South Africa becoming the first country in Olympic history to be excluded from the Olympic games. With South Africa excluded from the 1964 and 1968 Olympics, the country's sport-

48

ing future became an increasing state concern. By 1966, a Minister of Sport and Recreation had been appointed, while Prime Minister Vorster in 1967 announced South Africa's second policy statement concerning sport. This policy generally affirmed the earlier doctrine of 1956. Yet four years later in 1971 the same Prime Minister completely changed sporting policy. This change resulted from the events of 1970 which marked a crisis point in South African sporting history.

In 1970, the Council of Europe, the United Nations, the Commonwealth and the Supreme Council for Sport in Africa all condemned apartheid and sports under apartheid. The situation inside South Africa witnessed an escalation in conflict between the various sporting cultures as a result of the reorganisation of the non-racial sports movement in South Africa. The formation of the South African Non-Racial Sports Organisation (SASPO) in 1970 was closely followed by the emergence of the South African Council on Sport (SACOS) in 1971. In agreement with SACOS policy of non-collaboration with white sporting bodies, South Africa's non-racial tennis champion, Jasmut Dhiraj, comments:

> When we talk of non-racial sport, we are also talking
> of social and economic changes (from Archer and
> Bouillon, 1982: vi)

In conjunction with the events of the 1970s, Prime Minister Vorster unveiled a new 'multinational' sports policy (discussed in the next section of this chapter). Initially introduced in 1971, the policy took five years to be implemented in its final form. Yet the non-racial sports movement continually argued that the policy was merely an extension of South Africa's policy of separate development into sport. The policy was not one of multiracial integrated sport but one of multinational government-controlled sporting practice. Commenting on the situation during this particular period in history, the British Ministry of Sport affirmed in 1978 that the multinational sport policy continued to reflect the apartheid system:

> The Gleneagles[9] Agreement makes it quite clear that
> apartheid cannot be tolerated. The practice is

contrary to the principles of international sport and
therefore countries which allow the practice of
apartheid and racial discrimination in sport have
automatically excluded themselves from international
sport.[10]

Since international resistance to South African sport is discussed more extensively in the next chapter, I shall confine
myself here to making a few critical points in summary. Firstly,
until recently there were no laws forbidding mixed social sport
in South Africa. Even now, sporting legislation only indirectly
affects sporting practice, since, by and large, sport is governed
by the general laws upon which apartheid is built. Secondly,
the period since the late 1950s also witnessed the emergence of
a number of militant and non-racial sporting bodies which
have been a significant factor in determining the rest of the
world's sporting relationship with South Africa. The non-
racial sporting bodies have clearly emphasised that equality of
sporting opportunity will not come about through multiracial
sport but only through complete liberation.

I would argue that since its early beginnings, sport in South
Africa has served to differentiate further the inherent class
contradictions which have emerged from the South African
social formation. A number of socio-economic factors such as
education, standard of living and quality of life, as well as
public spending and government provision for sport, have influenced the development of sport. The ways in which sport is
experienced by the different cultural groupings are, in part,
determined by the organisational structure of South African
sport.

The organisation of sport in South Africa

The official organisation of South African sport is administered
through the Department of Sport and Recreation, founded in
1966. Since 1971 the Department has striven to implement a
number of sports policies in line with the government's official
multinational policy. According to the South African government,[11] multinational development can be implemented as described here:

In the light of the country's multi-national and
historical realities, the majority of whites are
convinced that relations between the white nation of
the Republic of South Africa and the various black
peoples ... cannot be satisfactorily regulated in a
single integrated superstate, but rather on the
historically tried basis of separate nation states, i.e. a
system of political independence coupled with
economic inter-dependence. (United Nations Report;
1980: 15)

Consequently, a number of white sporting organisations, such
as the South African Olympic Council, the National Games
Association, and the various governing bodies of white sport,[12]
work independently but are subject to state policy.[13]

Until 1979 the Organisation of African Sport came under
the general administration of the Department of Bantu Affairs
but it is now organised by a number of national tribal authorities under the general guidance of the Department of Sport
and Recreation. Similarly, coloured sport and Indian sport,
while they are administered through the Coloured Affairs Department and the Culture and Recreation Council, are
generally under the control of the Department of Sport and
Recreation.

Following the introduction of multinational sport in 1976,
some 'umbrella' sporting bodies were established in a number
of individual sports. As Hain points out, the development of
such bodies can be seen as part of an overall strategy, developed during the 1970s, designed to offset international criticism and preserve the core of apartheid (Hain, 1979: 183).
The term 'umbrella' was used to refer to those white sporting
bodies which encouraged a number of black sporting organisations to co-operate with white sporting policy in an attempt
to gain credibility for multinationalism. This involved a number of prominent white organisations appointing a non-white
president or official, while maintaining *de facto* control through
the white membership which provided financial support. Politically, these 'umbrella' bodies were used to portray an image
of integration and equality and to provide South African sport
with overall credibility. On 4 June 1976 Dr Koornhof (United
Nations, 8/80), Minister for Sport and Recreation, stated:

Certain kinds of sports such as athletics, rugby and
several others, have already established such umbrella
bodies. My Department and I are continually
working in this direction and we give valuable advice
and assistance to sports bodies, because it is in
accordance with policy that such umbrella bodies
should be established and through which various
population groups should be represented.

In resistance to white organised sport, a number of non-
racial sporting organisations have emerged during the latter
half of the twentieth century. Of specific interest is the South
African Council for Sport (SACOS) which was formed in
1971. Through SACOS a number of non-racial sporting organisations have emerged and are engaged in an ongoing struggle against white sport.[14] Since the roles of SACOS and other
resistance groups are considered in the next chapter, at this
point it is sufficient to report that the general theme uniting all
militant sporting groups is that 'you cannot have normal sport
in an abnormal society'. Consequently, as noted in a United
Nations Report (1980/8: 31):

SACOS in a declaration of its solidarity with the
Supreme Council for Sport in Africa rejects all forms
of racialism in sport and accepts a complete
moratorium on all sports tours to and from South
Africa until all the trappings of apartheid have been
removed from South African sport.

In short, South African sport is organised around a tripartite
structure which primarily involves white sporting bodies, black
sporting bodies and non-racial sporting bodies. Despite
attempts by non-racial sporting groups to expose South
Africa's sporting policy, state involvement in sport has continually attempted to portray an image of multiracial sport
through its multinational sports policy. In the context of this
study, it is argued that such a policy must be seen as an aspect
of the wider conjunctural response which has attempted to
defuse militancy through the creation of a black middle class
and by portraying an image of change to the outside world.

The emergence of a sporting policy

Sport in South African history has been determined primarily by general government policy rather than by specific legislation. The result is that direct government legislation concerning sport has a relatively short history. Invariably when reference has been made to sport, it has been in response to a period of crisis such as that of the 1970s.

Following the expulsion of the white South African Table Tennis Board from the International Table Tennis Federation in 1956, the first official government policy concerning sport emerged. In response to this expulsion, Dr Donges, Minister of the Interior, commented:

> Whites and non-whites should organise their sports
> separately. No mixed sport would be allowed within
> the borders of South Africa. Mixed teams going
> abroad should be avoided and international teams
> coming to South Africa to play against white South
> African teams should be all white according to South
> African custom. (Brickhill, 1976: 21)

At this point the government was already aware of the growing resistance, both internally and externally, to its racial sporting practice. A number of militant sporting organisations, as already mentioned, continually campaigned for the recognition of non-racial organisations and the expulsion of racist sporting organisations. This process of increasing resistance to apartheid through sport prompted Prime Minister Vorster to broadcast a second policy statement concerning sport in 1967:

> I want to make it quite clear that from South Africa's
> point of view no mixed sport between whites and
> non-whites will be practised locally, irrespective of
> the standard of proficiency of its participants ... the
> position is simply that whites practise and administer
> their sport separately, and that the other colour
> groups practise their sport separately. If any person,
> either locally or abroad, adopts the attitude that he
> will enter into relations with us only if we are
> prepared to jettison the separate practising of sport
> ... then I want to make it quite clear that no matter

53

how important those sporting relations are in my
view, I am not prepared to pay the price. (Brickhill,
1976: 21)

Four years later the same Prime Minister laid down the roots
of what today has become known as South Africa's multinational sports policy. However, this response must be seen in
the context of a chain of events which occurred during 1970.
The first of these was the expulsion in 1970 of South Africa
from the Olympic movement – the first time in history that
any country had been expelled. The second was that 1970
became known as the year of the boycott because of the massive
demonstrations which occurred in Britain, Ireland, Australia
and New Zealand. The third was that 1970 became the year of
judgment in which a number of political agencies such as the
United Nations, the Commonwealth and the Supreme Council
for Sport in Africa all condemned apartheid and apartheid
sport. The final event was, as Archer and Bouillon (1982: 206)
suggest, that 1970 was also the year of humiliation for South
Africa in that during that year it was banned from participating
in nine international sporting events and suspended from a
number of independent international sporting federations.

In response to this mounting international criticism and increasing sports isolation, Prime Minister Vorster announced
that blacks would be allowed to participate in a few sporting
events which would be termed 'multinational' or 'open international' events. In essence, this allowed the different racial
groups in South Africa to compete against each other as four
separate nations but only at the international level would mixed
sport be tolerated. No mixed sport or multiracial sport was to
be allowed at club or provincial level. While the shift in policy
was being portrayed internationally as a radical change in
policy, in practice the logic of apartheid was preserved in that
each racial group was allowed to develop its own separate
sporting relations with the proviso that the white administered
sporting bodies remained in overall control. The subtlety of
this position is outlined by Woods (1981: 125) who states that
the intention of the apparent shift in policy was:

> to make the international community believe that
> apartheid is being phased out while assuring the grass
> root followers that it is not.

While the initial multinational sports policy appeared in outline in 1971, it did not appear in its final format until 1976. The eight-point plan produced by Dr Koornhof was portrayed through the media as a major step in breaking down the walls of apartheid (see Appendix 2). Although the policy was publicised internationally as an indication of how South Africa was willing to move towards some form of multiracial society, perhaps the real meaning of the policy can be gleaned from the following statements in *Hansard* made by the Minister of Sport and Recreation between 1973 and 1979:

MAY 25TH 1973
separate participation in sport is a natural and more obvious outcome of the Government's policy of separate development. It is therefore wrong to speak of a new sports policy, or a different formula, or certain concessions.

And along the same lines . . .

the interpretation of the sports policy should constantly be consistent with the country's fundamental policy of separate development. If this is not done it is not only erroneous and meaningless, but also causes confusion.

MAY 18TH 1977
We want to compete internationally and we are going to compete internationally but let us admit here this afternoon that play and sport are strong enough to cause economic relations to flourish or collapse.

MAY 21ST 1979
The National Party reaffirms its well-known standpoints on sport as formulated in 1976 as the general and fundamental guidelines to be pursued wherever possible.

Several points can be drawn from these remarks. Firstly, they indicate the extent to which evolution of a 'multinational' sports policy must initially be viewed as an attempt by state personnel to influence and change international relations, both inside and outside the sporting arena. It is precisely the subordination of the South African economy to the world economy that makes sport such a crucial aspect of the conjunctural response. Sport is seen, as the 18 May passage suggests, as a primary mechanism for influencing favourable public opinion in a capitalist society that is heavily dependent upon foreign investment. Secondly, the emergence of this aspect of the conjunctural response does not relate simply to the sporting boycott but is also part of a response to a more widespread wave of hostility directed at South Africa after such incidents as the Sharpeville massacre in 1960 and the Soweto riots of 1976. Thirdly, in line with the *verligtes'* political philosophy, South Africa's multinational sports policy might be seen as an attempt to open up certain doors to an aspirant black middle class and negotiate away all but the core of apartheid. Finally, despite the lack of sporting legislation, sporting practice in South Africa is rigorously controlled through a number of core apartheid legislations which in general militate against mixed racial sport.

South African sport as it is specifically organised and structured by apartheid serves only to widen the inequalities between white and non-white culture. The inadequacy of South Africa's multinational sports policy, I believe, can be exposed through considering two of the major structural components influencing sporting practice, namely, economics and politics.

The political economy of South African sport

In recent years sponsorship has played an extensive role, not only in persuading black South Africans to succumb to the government's apartheid sports policy, but also in conferring international respectability through enticing international sportsmen and women from overseas to compete in South Africa. Furthermore, the marketing and commodification of South African sport has been one of the major factors determining sporting relations with South Africa, and the prevailing inequality of opportunity between white and non-white sport is perpetuated through such economic factors as existing systems of finance, facilities and sponsorship.

A major share of the blame for this inequality rests with the white government which generously subsidises white sport but pays little towards non-white sport. In *Facelift Apartheid* Seidman (1980) indicates the extent to which the central government's contributions to sport for the different races shows a disparity (see Table 3.1).

TABLE 3.1: Government financial expenditure on sport during 1979

	Percentage
Department of Sport and Recreation (white)	86.6
Department of Plural Relations and Development (non-white)	4.19
Department of Coloured Relations (non-white)	0.003
Department of Defence (non-white)	9.21

(*Adapted from Seidman, 1980: 31*)

A similar degree of inequality is indicated by Brickhill (1976: 19) in terms of provision for African and white sport for the year 1974-5. During this year public funds (taxes, revenues, etc.) contributed 7 per cent of the African sports budget. In contrast, public funds paid the whole of the white sports budget, in addition to the wealth that white sport acquired from private sources from club memberships, etc. Additional evidence concerning the total amount of public expenditure on sport has been summarised by Archer and Bouillon in the following table:

TABLE 3.2: Total public expenditures on sport (in rands)

Years	Whites	Africans	Coloureds	Indians
1965–72	2,708.900	?	102,150	?
1974–75	1,217,612	464,317	333,792	?
1975–76	1,417,609	415,439	449,112	20,300
1977–78	1,585,724	495,394	187,420	?

(*Adapted from Archer and Bouillon, 1982: 168*)

The inequitable distribution of central and local funding has also affected the level of sporting provision for the different ethnic cultures. Again Africans suffer, as they do in all spheres, more than any other group. Since Africans do not have any form of control over sporting facilities they are entirely dependent upon white organisations and white municipalities for funding. No overall survey of sports facilities available to different groups in South Africa has ever been published and yet there is still ample evidence[15] to suggest that subordinate cultural groups, particularly African cultures, receive inadequate provision. For instance, Brickhill (1976: 70) notes that there are a number of disparities in terms of sports grounds and swimming baths which are provided for in white planning programmes for white areas and the facilities available in the black townships of Umlazi, Soweto and Guguletu. The inference is that in non-white areas, far too many people were expected to use far too few facilities.

Similar conclusions can be drawn from the Taljaard (1981: 97) survey into the provision of parks, sports and recreation amenities for the different racial groups in the Cape Province. The Taljaard study suggested that in agreement with the 1978 De Hoek Report, there was an appreciable difference in the quality of existing facilities provided for whites and non-whites. Secondly, it was argued that the provision of adequate sporting facilities in non-white areas should be matched by providing better housing, sewage and electricity so that the quality of life could be improved. Finally, it was noted that a number of additional factors such as accessibility in terms of transport, time available for leisure, cost factors and choice of activity also disadvantaged the non-white groups in the Cape Province.

Perhaps the most significant economic factor in relation to South African sport is the marketing of South African sport abroad through sponsorship, propaganda and lucrative bonuses to willing participants. The specialist role of the media in marketing sport cannot be over-emphasised. Newspapers and broadcasting stations have provided an indispensable means of advertising games and reinforcing the ideology of multiracial sport in an effort to encourage the governing bodies of sport to accept South Africa back into the sporting world. During the build-up to the Moscow Olympics the following statement appeared in *The Sunday Times* (26 February 1980):

> While the dispute rages over the Moscow Olympics,
> no one suggests that Soviet athletes should be
> penalised .... However, with South Africa, it is the

athletes themselves who are denied, by the
International Olympic Committee's boycott, the
ultimate goal of competing internationally. Why?
Because it is alleged that South Africa's non-racial
policies deny equal opportunities to black athletes.
Today this is simply untrue; the controlling bodies of
sport in South Africa are autonomous.

The statement is significant for two main reasons; firstly it provides a typical example of South African propaganda overseas, and secondly, it demonstrates the extent to which international relations are in part determined and influenced by false information. The ill-informed reader, for instance, would fail to distinguish between non-racial and multinational sports policies.

The power of South African capital, in particular commercial sponsorship, has, since 1970, played a significant part in influencing sporting relations with South Africa. It can be argued that, like any company investment, this is legitimate purely in terms of profit and is therefore non-political. Because the operations of private companies are secret it would be impossible to prove that any company's operations were politically motivated but it is significant that during the last decade there has been a growing bond between sponsorship and international sporting contacts with South Africa.

South African capital has been used in two major ways, with the primary one being aimed at the production of overseas sporting contacts. There is ample evidence[16] to underpin the assumption that South African capital has been heavily involved in enticing overseas sportsmen and women to visit South Africa. For instance, the Access[17] Report into the 1981 Springbok rugby tour of the United States revealed that the hosts, Eastern Rugby Union (ERU), had received some 75,000 dollars from various South African sources to promote the tour. Furthermore, the day after the tour was announced, it was disclosed that the ERU had sought funds from Citibank, one of the largest US lenders to South Africa. More specifically, the ERU solicited funds from some 300 US corporations on the promise that corporations who helped to sponsor the tour would be looked upon favourably in terms of South African contracts (Lapchick, 1981).

During the first half of 1982 South African companies invested some 5 million dollars in attracting overseas golfers, cricketers, swimmers and football players to the country. By far the largest single sponsor of apartheid sport in the past has been the South African Breweries. In conjunction with the Southern Sun Hotel Group, the South African Breweries financed the English cricket tour and British football[18] venture during July 1982. Yet despite the attraction of such lucrative offers, a number of athletes have opted out of South African competitions.

The United Nations register of sporting contacts with South Africa has forced many prospective sports visitors to reconsider the question of sporting contacts with South Africa. Several sportsmen and women[19] have come to realise the extent to which such outside contact can be used by South Africa to advertise apartheid policy internationally.

A second way in which South African capital is used in the sporting context is to persuade a number of black Africans to co-operate within the framework of multinational sport. As Ramsamy (1982: 78) indicates, sponsors[20] play a large part in luring black South African sportsmen and women into joint racial leagues or government-instigated multinational competitions. Commenting on those black Africans who compromise, Hassan Howa, former President of SACOS, explains:

> People who are compromising in sport all of a
> sudden take a huge leap in their everyday lives,
> financially and otherwise. I know of several
> administrators who were bankrupt at one stage and
> who are very rich men today. (*Rand Daily Mail*, 6
> April, 1978.)

It has been argued that an analysis of the South African sporting economy dispels the myth that sport in South Africa provides for equality of opportunity or sporting chance. Yet government policy since 1976 has continually emphasised the importance of multinational sport at an international level. What a number of international observers forget is that sport in South Africa is not primarily determined by sporting legislation but by general government policy. It is the apartheid law itself which serves to perpetuate and institutionalise the inequalities in sport. In the final part of this chapter, the ways in which a number of apartheid laws militate against multiracial sport are demonstrated.

As stated earlier, there is not any specific law in South Africa which directly prohibits mixed sport. There are, however, certain laws which in effect rigorously control sporting practice. Some of these are pointed out by Ramsamy in his book, *Apartheid: The Real Hurdle* (1982). Here are some examples:

1 The Population Registration Act of 1950. This Act provides for a rigid system of classification according to race.
2 The Group Areas Act of 1966. It is this Act which divides South Africa into areas of occupancy and residency according to race.
3 The Reservation of Separate Amenities Act of 1953. This Act permits owners of property to evict or exclude members of certain races from premises. It, for instance, specifically segregates post offices, stadiums, parks, swimming baths and libraries.
4 The Native Law Amendments Act of 1957. This Act provides for the withholding of permission for Africans to attend gatherings outside their own native residential area.

In effect, these laws militate against a truly non-racial sporting practice. Firstly, the Population Registration Act determines sporting categories and organisations on the basis of race. Secondly, the Group Areas Act hinders free travel to matches and competitions outside an individual's area of residence. Thirdly, the Separate Amenities Act still segregates certain facilities in terms of total usage in some cases, e.g. private clubs in particular, and partial usage in others, and the hours that specific races can use certain facilities. However, the major significance of the Act is that it gives owners and management the power to evict occupants on racial grounds. Finally, the Native Law Amendments Act provides a further means of control over truly non-racial sporting practice. Only in special cases are these laws relaxed, e.g. multinationally endorsed international events.

The absence of legislation which explicitly prevents mixed

racial sport has had a number of advantages for the South African government. It has meant that internally sport can still be directly controlled through apartheid legislation but at the same time it has been possible for white sports administrators to gain several dispensations with regard to international sport. Thus, realising the value of inviting black sporting celebrities to South Africa, the South African government amended a number of apartheid laws to accommodate such visitors. For instance, during 1981–2 the government introduced a number of legal dispensations for sport, modifying the Liquor Amendments Act, the Group Areas Act and the Native Urban Areas Consolidation Act. The amendments to these Acts enable black sporting visitors to be classified as 'honorary white citizens' while they are competing in South Africa. The shallowness of these dispensations is exposed by Ramsamy (1982: 38) who points out that the mixing of races which is provided for by these amendments only extends to the duration of the event and no further. And so, for instance, a black sportsman or sportswoman might be given permission to take part in a swimming competition in a pool for whites only and yet not be allowed to use the same pool after the event for recreational swimming or even for training.

The success of multinational sport and the subsequent changes in legislation to accommodate the policy have thus rested upon a degree of confusion being perpetuated internationally between the terms 'multinational' and 'multiracial'. Internationally, sport under apartheid has been marketed as multiracial yet internally, sport for the majority of non-white Africans is controlled through a number of economic and political factors and is not multiracial. By tolerating a degree of mixed racial sport at the international level, the government has attempted to satisfy both the demands of the critics abroad and the white political minority at home. The latter are led to believe that the status quo will be maintained while the former are encouraged to believe that sport in South Africa has been normalised.

This chapter has been concerned with an attempt to expose the ideology of multiracial sport through the consideration of a number of historical and political economic factors. In the next chapter I take up the related theme of tracing the struggle for black recognition through non-racial sport. This second theme specifically looks at the way in which sport might be used as part of a total strategy of resistance aimed at bringing about social change in South Africa. Sport may not seem central to the liberation of the country from apartheid and so resistance through sport may seem secondary to the resistance struggles which involve broader liberation forces. Yet popular struggles invariably involve cultural projects as part of their broader front. In South Africa, political front movements such as the African National Congress (ANC), the Pan Africanist Congress (PAC) and the South African Communist Party (SACP) have differed in their approach to political liberation and oppositional cultural production. The major rift revolves around whether class or nation should be the driving force in social change.

FOUR
SPORT AND
RESISTANCE

This work has indicated the dialectical relationship which has evolved between some of the organic and the conjunctural forces at play within the South African social formation. In the short term it is against the conjunctural terrain that one should analyse the strategies of forces of opposition. The struggle for sporting hegemony within South Africa has been largely influenced by the non-racial sporting movement which has continually confronted the issues surrounding multinational sporting development. The struggle through sport is only part of the struggle mounted by the oppositional forces such as AZAPO, SAN-ROC, BCM, and ANC. In this chapter it is argued that sporting resistance ought to be seen as part of a total strategy mounted by the oppressed cultures in opposition to the dominant conjunctural response.

The liberation movement of the 1980s has been led by the exiled ANC. However, a number of revolutionary factions have operated within South Africa. The major problem concerning solidarity between the various factions has been a fundamental disagreement about the precise nature of the national liberation struggle. AZAPO and the remnants of the banned BCM and PAC forces have argued that the future of Azania[1] lies not through a working-class struggle arising out of social relations of production, but through African nationalism alone. Thus Biko[2] (1979:134–36) dismissed white Marxists who say that the situation is a class struggle rather than a racial struggle. The position taken by the latter forces of opposition has been strongly influenced by the writings of Franz Fanon. It is within the context of a discussion of broader liberation strategies that resistance against white sporting hegemony is discussed in this chapter.

Resistance through sport

South Africa is unusual and perhaps unique in that sport has become an overtly open object of civil struggle. The various white sporting policies have met with considerable internal and external resistance.[3] Aiming to create sporting practice free from all forms of racism, including the racism inherent in multinationalism, black sporting resistance internally has been expressed during the 1980s through SACOS. While a number of sporting organisations have historically compromised their demands the strength of SACOS as a sporting mode of resistance lies in its refusal to separate sporting demands from broader demands for social change. Writing in *The South African Game* (1982: 307) Archer and Bouillon cite Middleton's[4] explanation of the strategy behind the hard line approach taken by SACOS:

> I believe, gentlemen, that at least for the time being and particularly in the absence of any form of democracy in this country, that we must use all types of platforms created for us. The difference being that we use these platforms on our own terms, as platforms of free expression, to confront and embarrass the whole system. I agree that anybody using these created platforms for his own ends[5] and without exposing the situation has no right to claim or belong to any of our non-racial organisations.

The level of sporting consciousness expressed by SACOS's affiliates has evolved historically through a number of internal sporting struggles. African sporting resistance originally found solidarity in SASA and SAN-ROC, with the creation of SASA in 1958 marking the beginning of the non-racial sports movement. By providing a source of unification in purely sporting terms, SASA permitted black sporting culture to support the broader struggle against apartheid.[6] While SASA provided a source of solidarity, the same could not be said of the broader liberation forces which experienced a major split during the second half of the 1950s.

Historically, the ANC movement exemplified many of the contradictory tensions which the revolutionary movement in South Africa is currently facing. While the initial ANC strategy was essentially reformist, there was within it a more militant approach stemming from the trade union movement under the leadership of Clements Kadalie.[7] Only after the 1946 mine workers' strike did the national movement, represented by the ANC, and working-class groups, represented by SACTU, begin to link up more effectively. On 26 June 1955 SACTU and the ANC formed an alliance, which immediately increased the impact of SACP in drawing the ANC movement towards a more proletarian line of action. The coalition between the philosophically[8] opposing forces found its expression in the Freedom Charter adopted in 1956. The main points, write Karis and Carter (1972, 3:205), of the Charter were:

1   All national groups shall have equal rights.
2   All national groups will be protected by law against insults to their race and national pride.
3   All people shall have equal rights to use their own language and to develop their own folk culture and customs.
4   The preaching and practice of national, race or colour discrimination and contempt shall be a punishable crime.
5   All apartheid laws and practices shall be set aside.

For the militant national fraction of the ANC the Freedom Charter marked a shift[9] in policy. The Charter marked a noticeable swing towards a more socialist approach and stressed the need for unity among the African majority with regard to the nature of the liberation process. Instead of advocating outright black majority rule, the ANC, for the time being, talked in terms of a multiracial state. Although the ANC clearly declared that South Africa belonged to all that lived in it, Mandela (1978: 55) took care to explain that support for the Charter was by no means a blueprint for a completely socialist state.

The coalition was not without its critics in the liberation movement. Hard-line Africans agitated against the alliance on a number of grounds. Firstly, they thought it meant the ANC was turning away from African nationalism as the main catalyst for struggle. Secondly, they were unhappy with the growing influence of the white-oriented SACP. Thirdly, they attacked the phrase that South Africa belonged to all who live in the country, black and white; and finally, they criticised the ANC's lack of concrete plans for mobilising the African masses into action.

By the end of the 1950s both the ANC and SASA succeeded in extending resistance to apartheid into a number of areas. The tactics used by SASA in extending black resistance into sport were similar to those used by the ANC. As Archer and Bouillon (1982: 192) say:

> The tactics of civil disobedience adopted by
> sportsmen were also those used by the ANC....
> Furthermore, because it was played by the petty
> bourgeoisie and by the urban workers ... sport
> provided a particularly favourable ground upon
> which to attack apartheid.

While SASA remained politically active and united during the later part of the 1950s, the rift along nationalist and socialist lines within the ANC led to a split in 1959. The split resulted in the formation of the PAC, who vowed to reinforce the nationalist aspirations of the vast majority of the oppressed culture. The general positions were set out by Robert Sobukwe at the PAC's Inaugural Convention:

> We aim politically at government of the Africans by
> the Africans, for the Africans, with everybody who
> owes his own loyalty to Africa and who is prepared
> to accept the democratic rule of an African being
> regarded as African (from No Sizwe, 1979: 117).

By December 1959 the PAC leadership had decided that it was time to openly challenge white authority rule and called for a broad campaign of civil disobedience against the pass laws. This marked the beginning of a campaign against oppression which ended in the Sharpeville riots of 1960 (see Chapter 2). The tide of African militancy was cut short following the repressive state crackdown after Sharpeville. The core of ANC and PAC leaders were either arrested or forced into exile.

As a result of the dominant cultural response to the Sharpeville riots SASA remained one of the few avenues for protest against apartheid during the 1960s. All other militant organisations had either been banned or destroyed. It is all the more significant, therefore, that at the time when the ANC and PAC leadership were arrested, SASA created a further militant sporting organisation, namely SAN-ROC. The formation of SAN-ROC in 1962 stemmed from SASA's continual failure to win support from the International Olympic Committee (IOC). Under the leadership of Denis Brutus, SAN-ROC emerged as the symbol[10] of struggle for non-racial sport in South Africa. The movement's specific policy was to expose racial domination wherever possible in sport and to force the IOC to expel South Africa from the Olympic Movement.

Brutus (1972: 156) notes that SAN-ROC's existence within South Africa was relatively short-lived since within two years of its creations, its leading members[11] 'had been exiled and its activities suspended within South Africa'. Yet it was during this period of repression that SAN-ROC scored its first major victory in that the IOC in 1964 banned South African athletes from participating in the Olympic Games in Tokyo. As Brickhill (1976: 11) records, the shock to the white public, accustomed to free participation in world sports, was considerable. More shocks were to come.

The relatively trouble-free time of the 1960s was not to last for long. During the 1960s and early 1970s the initiative lay primarily with the groups of black students who found expression through the leadership of Steve Biko. The student organisations gave birth to a number of militant organisations. Their message, 'black man, you are on your own', articulated for many the frustrations of a generation of young blacks whose sole experience was that of apartheid. While the BCM ideologically laid the roots for the Soweto uprising of 1976, it subsequently bore the brunt of the repression that followed and culminated in the death of Steve Biko.[12]

However, the resistance movement was not forced entirely underground. In May 1978 the BCM sought to regroup with AZAPO with the aim of specifically organising black workers to take militant action through strikes. Despite the emergence of a number of internal resistance movements during the 1970s and 1980s, the exiled ANC movement is still viewed as the major mobilising force on the liberation front. According to Saul and Gelb (1981: 139) there are two basic reasons for the ANC having this sort of gravitational pull. One important reason is the ANC's growing military capacity. The dramatic acts of sabotage at the Sasolburg oil storage facilities in 1980 forced the Minister of Police to proclaim that ANC forces were everywhere in South Africa. A second, less tangible, but equally important, factor is the movement's depth of history and its involvement with the liberation struggle since its inception in 1912.

Just as the ANC continued to function from exile, so did SAN-ROC. By 1965 SAN-ROC had again become the dominant force within the non-racial sports movement. Operating from London, the group continued to agitate against white sporting federations and white South African society in general.

With SAN-ROC in exile, the non-racial sporting movement in South Africa was not only deprived of a means of solidarity but was subjected to a campaign waged against them by the white associations and co-ordinated by the government. This campaign formed the basis of what was later to become multinational sport. It revolved around three axial principles: (1) creation of separate Indian, coloured and African associations; (2) to finance and promote the emergence of a small black sporting elite; (3) to force this black elite to support the status quo and official apartheid policies. This move effectively deprived the non-racial sports movement inside South Africa of finance, facilities and unification.

Yet the move to form non-racial sporting organisations as opposed to black sporting organisations proved to be significant in that it significantly increased the strength of the sporting resistance movement. Up until that point, the only political weapon available was a plea for the expulsion of the white sporting federations. The removal of a discriminatory policy against white subjects meant that the black sporting organisations could now expand their demands in calling not only for the expulsion of white sporting federations but also for the international recognition of non-racial sporting federations.

While the policy of non-racial sport in principle was adhered to by the black oppressed sporting culture, in practice it meant the near-cessation of nearly all sporting activity. Despite major problems[13] facing the movement, in theory non-racial sport as a political weapon was preserved. The position of the non-racial bodies was very much in line with the position adopted by the non-racial South African Amateur Swimming Federation:

> Our goal is complete non-racial swimming at every
> level in the country administered by a single, truly
> non-racial swimming organisation, not the useless,
> ineffective and misleading body like the Amateur
> Aquatics Federation of South Africa. (United
> Nations, 1980/8: 8)

With SAN-ROC in exile, the primary task of the non-racial movement was simply to survive against the push for multi national sport. Despondent with the lack of progress towards the non-racial sport, representatives from a number of national sports organisations gathered in Durban during September 1970 to form the South African Non-Racial Sports Organisation (SASPO). The formation of SASPO again brought a degree of internal solidarity to the non-racial movement. However, while continually denouncing South African sports policy the organisation was willing to collaborate with white organisations on a number of issues. It is of no small significance that during the same period the BCM was calling for the re-establishment of black identity and for an end to black recognition and relations with white culture. As Biko (1979: 63–4) argued:

> The biggest mistake the black world ever made was
> to assume that whoever opposed apartheid was an
> ally. For a long time the black world has been
> looking at the governing party and not so much at
> the whole power structure as the object of their rage.
> In a sense the very political vocabulary that the
> blacks have used has been inherited from the liberals.

The awakening of black consciousness strongly affected the direction of the non-racial sports resistance in that black athletes called for a more aggressive approach to multinational sports. In March 1979 the formation of the South African Council on Sport (SACOS) provided black sporting culture with a more militant resistance movement. As already mentioned, the appeal of SACOS lay in its policy of no negotiation, and a declaration of solidarity among non-racial sports organisations, until all the symbols of apartheid had been removed not only from South African sport but also from South African society. Indeed, the aggressive approach adopted by SACOS worried some of its own members who felt that the inflexible approach to radical policies might sever the movement from the mass of African sportsmen and women.[14]

The resistance to multinationalism from SACOS revolved around four key issues. Firstly, the movement took issue against the permit system which requires non-whites to be in possession of sporting permits if they are playing any form of multinational sport. Any sports event which is not multinational, i.e. government endorsed[15] is refused a permit. If a black sports body wishes to defy government policy and hold a mixed sport event, its officials are politely warned about the consequences.[16] In a pamphlet issued to all black athletes in 1978, SACOS not only called for athletes to shed their slave mentality but to refuse to play sport under permit conditions since it deprives athletes of their human rights as South Africans (United Nations, 1980/8: 20).

Secondly, SACOS stood firm around the 'double standards resolution' which served as a means of maintaining cohesion among truly non-racial organisations. The resolution banned black individuals who collaborated with multinational sport in any form from becoming SACOS members. Simply, this meant that any affiliate to SACOS in one code[17] or sport could not belong to a racial unit in another code or sport, e.g. multinational organisations. Again the policy of non-collaboration must be seen within the broader context of the liberation struggle. In both cases other forms of recourse, negotiation, protest, and critical co-operation have been frustrated or crushed by the authorities. Blacks have consistently been pressed by the multinational sporting organisations to concede the principle of racial equality, over which they refuse to make concessions.

Thirdly, SACOS took issue over the unequal distribution of sponsorship money in sport (see Chapter 3). This was very much in line with SACOS's policy of non-negotiation with the apartheid system in any shape or form. Since the major sponsorship companies derived their profits from black labour, sponsored sport served only to support the apartheid formation. SACOS's policy in this area has been confined to a negative criticism of unequal sponsorship distribution between the tripartite sports system.

Finally, SACOS called for a complete ban on international sporting relations with South Africa until the existing social formation is abolished and non-racial sporting practice universally accepted. The commitment of non-racial sportsmen and sportswomen is highlighted by SACOS resolutions which ban all tours by non-racial, as well as racial, associations. The position taken by SACOS over international sporting relations has been strengthened by the international backing of its policies. For instance, the United Nations ban on sporting contact with South Africa issued on 24 October 1980 included the compilation of a list of all those countries who maintained sporting contact with South Africa. According to a United Nations press release (5/80):

> The director of the centre against apartheid ...
> announced today that in accordance with the
> decisions made by the special committee, the centre
> has initiated a compilation of a register of sportsmen,
> sports administrators and others who flagrantly
> violated the sports boycott against South Africa.

The success of the international boycott has revolved around several influential pieces of legislation, none more so than the Gleneagles Agreement signed by all the heads of Commonwealth countries on 15 June 1977. However, while the international boycott has served to bring pressure to bear on South Africa and provided SACOS members with a certain degree of security from repression, sporting literature, I believe, has tended to over-emphasise the part played by the international boycott at the expense of the struggles waged by the sporting proletariat within South Africa.

While the importance of the international boycott should not be underestimated, the futility of sporting sanctions alone can be criticised on a number of grounds. Firstly, as already pointed out, while the international boycott has provided the non-racial movement with some degree of political leverage, it has also tended to undermine the efforts of the international resistance movements in forcing change in South Africa. Secondly, although a number of western and eastern countries have implemented sporting sanctions, the same countries such as Britain, America, Japan and West Germany have also continued to enter into political and economic trade negotiations with South Africa. Finally, if liberation from apartheid is to materialise or even capitalise on the current organic crisis, it will result not from the isolated efforts of sporting resistance movements, but from a total strategy involving the broader liberation forces. To reiterate Archer and Bouillon (1982, 307):

> Sport and sporting policy is marginal in that
> relatively few Africans play sport, which means that
> even if sport were completely integrated, it would
> have little effect on the well-being of the majority,
> who would still be confined to the compounds,
> townships and bantustans.

The remainder of this chapter takes up the question of sport's centrality to popular struggle in South Africa in the context of the broader problems of resistance movements.

Sport, hegemony and the problems of popular struggle

Class and cultural struggle over capitalism in South Africa are so closely bound up with that of racial oppression that it is almost impossible to separate the struggle against apartheid from the struggle against class domination.[18] The dialectic between nationalism and socialism is evident in the two-stage strategy adopted by the ANC and the SACP – first, the national democratic revolution against apartheid and then the socialist revolution against capitalism. AZAPO and the remnants of the PAC and the BCM on the other hand have argued that the only path to revolution is the national path. PAC took their initial inspiration from Anton Lembewe (cited in Gerhart, 1978: 60) who wrote in 1946:

> Africa is a black man's country. The basis of national
> unity is the nationalistic feeling of South Africans,
> the feeling of being Africans, irrespective of tribal

connection, social status, educational attainment or
economic class.

The general underlying philosophy behind the PAC resistance movement in particular has been put forward in the writings of Franz Fanon.[19] Yet a concentration on Fanon's writings
alone undermines the broader class and cultural struggles that
have been highlighted in this study. Suffice it to say that
Fanon's thesis in *The Wretched of the Earth* (1982) touches on
a number of themes relevant to South African struggles such
as ideology of violence and the notion of spontaneous resistance. However, the attraction of Gramsci's notion of hegemony
and the way in which it is used in this study is that all forms
of popular struggle must be seen within a totality – a totality
which merges into a counter-hegemonic struggle, a popular
struggle consisting of number of cultural forces. Consider some
examples of such cultural forces and struggles.

A first example is the trade union movement and the
prominent struggles waged at the point of production. The
escalation in working-class action and industrial dispute
reached new heights in 1980. Implicit in the perspective argued
for here is an awareness of the importance of the black trade
union movement. It is only out of a successful struggle around
the mode of production that black workers can acquire further
consciousness. Yet the struggle over consciousness must be
seen as a political and cultural project and should not be limited to the industrial sphere.

In addition to industrial strikes are classroom boycotts, con-
sumer boycotts, and mass demonstrations and sporadic community struggles such as those in Cape Town during 1980.
Even if some of these community struggles have not linked up
directly with industrial strikes and trade union action the
overall result is one of pressure on the existing regime. Even
stronger pressure comes from the liberation forces such as the
ANC, the PAC and the BCM to name but a few. Here again
it must be emphasised that to date the success of the liberation
forces as a whole has been severely hampered as a result of the
diversification and a lack of totality and unification concerning
strategy, methodology and action.

The ANC's unconditional acceptance of violence has tended
to undermine the repertoire of tactics and strategies open to

the liberation armies. In particular, it fails to recognise the success of the African trade union movement in organising passive mass strikes (Appendix 1). The PAC and BCM on the other hand have clearly distinguished national and racial questions above all other forms of struggle. While Fanon adopts the position that colonised countries can only be seen as being polarised into two radically conflicting groups, namely the oppressors and the oppressed, this question ignores questions about the nature of a society's basic relations of production. Many would argue that political and economic struggles among different social groups must primarily be seen as class struggles arising out of the social relations of production.

Finally, the question must be asked: 'Where does sport fit into all of this?' As argued in Chapter 1, it is not necessary to consider broader forms of cultural struggle as peripheral or meaningless. Sport as part of cultural struggle in South Africa is important for two main reasons: (1) the way in which it is used by the state as a means of suggesting to the rest of the world that egalitarian change has taken place in South Africa. Sport itself has been taken into the political domain by the dominant white culture; (2) the way in which resistance to white sporting hegemony has been contested, struggled and fought for through the non-racial sporting movements. Since very few avenues of protest exist in South Africa, in comparison to western countries, the core of cultural activity becomes even more important.

Yet, sporting counter-hegemony has also been undermined as a result of the inflexible radical policies adopted by SACOS. Furthermore, external efforts concerning the international boycott have tended to deflect attention away from the internal struggles involving SACOS and the non-racial sporting movement in general.

The notion of Gramsci's modern party which links together the idea of counter-hegemonic struggles and national popular struggles provides a sense of totality and unification missing from the South African situation.

In *Gramsci's Marxism*, Boggs (1980) distinguishes between Lenin and Gramsci. For Gramsci, politics was deeply embedded in all aspects of the collective revolutionary struggle, as part of an ensemble of social relations. While Gramsci referred to the dialectical process between the organic and the conjunctural, Lenin tended to have a political fixation on the conjunctural aspect of revolutionary struggle. The main criticism from Gramsci's conception was that Lenin's notion of politics appeared to be undialectical.[20] The attractiveness of Gramsci's conception of a revolutionary party is that while emphasising the primacy of politics during moments of crisis it was within a totality encompassing both the organic and conjunctural aspects of struggle.

Gramsci's model of revolutionary transformation departed significantly from Lenin's as a result of Gramsci's emphasis upon hegemony.[21] At the core of these crucial differences is Gramsci's dual perspective, outlined in Chapter 1, namely the organic and conjunctural dimensions of change. As Boggs (1980: 115) indicates:

> The Gramscian model was dialectical in that it
> specified a reciprocal interaction between the organic
> and conjunctural and between the party and the
> larger complex of social groups which make up the
> total milieu.

The conception of totality is what distinguishes Gramsci's theory of the revolutionary party most clearly. What he formulated was a model of political organisation rooted in the everyday social life and formed organically through popular struggle, rather than a strict primacy of politics over the social sphere. It is in this sense that Gramsci (1980: 151) wrote:

> The history of a party can only be the history of a
> particular social group. But this group is not isolated.
> It has friends, kindred groups, opponents, enemies.

In the South African situation, the central role of such a party would be to co-ordinate and direct the different national, socialist and popular struggles taking place. Such a party formed through an interaction between leadership and masses must acknowledge the working-class character of the South African revolution and a willingness to use a variety of methods in the struggle against apartheid. This could only happen, writes Callinicos (1981: 166), if sections of the black resistance were prepared to enter into coalitions with the socialist movement and to involve themselves in the struggles in the factories and the mines. To Callinicos's argument I would add that such coalitions would also need to include groups engaged in other forms of struggle such as women's groups, education groups, and the non-racial sports movement.

FIVE

CONCLUSIONS

The fact that in 1984 liberal-minded politicians, sports officials, players and individuals still argue that the apartheid regime has made tremendous efforts to desegregate areas of cultural significance such as sport is indicative of the South African state's ability to portray an ideology of multiracialism. This ability, however, should not obscure several points. Firstly, that South Africa is a capitalist social formation in which the economy has been greatly affected by the international crisis of capitalism that has developed since the mid-1970s. Added to this, however, the proletarianisation of black workers has led to the development of consciousness among a black working-class culture that has substantially threatened the hegemony of the white dominant class. The result is not some transitory or passing economic crisis of capitalism; rather it is a deeply rooted, organic crisis. Secondly, the conjunctural response of the dominant white minority serves only to underline that the crisis is in fact organic. Thirdly, sport, more than any other aspect of the conjunctural response, has been used as one of the primary mechanisms of portraying an ideology of change to the rest of the world. Finally, while struggle over sport is not sufficient in itself to the process of liberation from apartheid, sporting resistance can potentially be integrated into a total strategy involving broader forces of resistance. As a part of the summary and conclusion to this study each of these points should be noted in more detail.

The manifestations of South Africa's economic crisis are to be seen in a number of factors, such as a negative growth of the economy, massive and rising unemployment, the ever-present adverse balance of payments and the decline of both foreign and local investment in the private sector (see Wolpe, 1983). A boom in the price of gold during the late 1970s and the 1980s proved to be only a temporary respite for the regime. As the *Financial Mail* (6 October 1982) reported at the end of 1982, the balance of payments current account was transferred from a surplus of almost R3 billion in 1979 to a deficit of almost R3.7 billion in 1981. The deficit is now running at an annual rate of R5.4 billion. Similarly, foreign investment and economic growth are once more on the decline.

Furthermore, a number of problems specific to South Africa have served only to exacerbate the problem. In particular, the continuing process of capital accumulation has had contradictory effects. Most noticeably, it has generated a more powerful demand for a more skilled black labour force, because the need for such workers cannot be met from the white or immigrant population. This shortage of skilled labour has strengthened the position of the black labour movement to extract reforms. Yet the creation of a black working class has also created the conditions for a coalescence of class and trade union consciousness among the workers that threatens the dominant set of class relations.

As South African capitalism developed, blacks formed numerous groups, political, cultural and trade union, to try to advance their struggle for class and national emancipation. Scarcely a decade went by, since the turn of the century, without a major battle being fought; the mass black demonstrations and strikes in the 1910s, the meteoric growth of African unionisation in the 1920s, attempts at forging broad African unity in the 1930s, work stoppages, urban riots and mass protest campaigns of the 1940s, boycotts, general strikes and massive civil disobedience actions of the 1950s, widespread rebellion following the Sharpeville masacre of the 1960s, labour unrest and student rebellions of the 1970s, and finally, bombings and labour tensions which have characterised the early part of the 1980s.

It is precisely this continuing development of class and racial consciousness, arising in part from the relations of production, which have turned the initial economic crisis facing South Africa into an organic crisis. The conjunctural response of the dominant white minority underlines the fact that a deep crisis does indeed exist. As noted at the outset of this study, the conjunctural does not merely emerge, it is constructed by the dominant culture and, as such, must not be seen as a reflection of the crisis but as a response to it. What defines the conjunctural is not merely the given economic conditions, but the incessant and continuous efforts being made to preserve and defend the status quo in the face of opposition.

A number of new programmes and policies were introduced under Prime Minister Botha. Firstly, the Riekert Report, published in May 1979, attempted to defuse black militancy and cure the shortage of skilled labour through the creation of an incorporated black middle class. Secondly, the suggestions of the Riekert Report complemented those of the Wiehahn Commission which suggested that Africans should be permitted to form registered trade unions under the Industrial Conciliation Act. The purpose of encouraging registration lay not so much in promoting equality, but rather in identifying, through registration, sectors of the black militant majority. While the measures adopted by the state have been aimed at restructuring class relations, they have also opened up terrains of political struggle which were simply not available during the 1960s. As Bose (1982) explains, ideological reform does not merely mask continued violent domination, it also signals the development of new, or reinstated, areas of political struggle, such as the trade union front, education and the student movement and the struggle for women's rights, to name but a few of the areas. In short, the political opposition has secured and struggled over a number of terrains of political action which, despite a degree of state interference, continue as important bases of mobilisation.

It is within this area of the conjunctural, I have argued, that South Africa's sporting policies can be situated. While the ideology of multinational sport has suggested that radical change has taken place, in practice, South African sport serves only to maintain the gap between white and non-white cultures. The success of multinational sport and the subsequent changes in legislation to accommodate the policy have rested upon a degree of confusion being perpetuated between the terms 'multinational' and 'multiracial'. Internationally, sport under apartheid has been marketed as multiracial, while internally sport for the majority of Africans is controlled through a number of economic and political factors and strategies which militate against the free playing of multiracial sport.

In terms of economic expenditure, facilities and sponsorship, a gross inequality exists between the four racial groups. The major criticism lies in the fact that sport in South Africa is not primarily determined by sporting legislation but by general economic conditions and government policy. It is the unique interaction of apartheid law with the social relations of South African capitalism which serves to institutionalise the inequalities in sporting practice. When we talk of sporting change in South Africa, we are therefore talking about socio-economic and political changes. The emergence of multinational sport must not give rise to the idea that such a development evolved without a struggle. The struggle over a white sporting hegemony has always been active, a struggle which in the 1980s has been expressed through the non-racial sports movement, SACOS.

A number of sporting resistance movements, such as SASA and SAN-ROC, at various historical moments have provided the non-racial movement with a source of solidarity. However, the distinctiveness of SACOS as a forum for resistance lies in the fact that while other sporting organisations have historically compromised their demands, SACOS has continually refused to separate sporting demands from broader demands for social change.

I have argued that while the importance of sporting resistance should not be underestimated, sporting resistance alone will not bring about liberation from apartheid. If liberation from apartheid is to materialise from the current organic crisis it will result not from the isolated efforts of the non-racial sports movement, but from a total strategy involving the broader liberation forces. As I have suggested in Chapter 2, it is not necessary merely to hypothesise about the existence of revolutionary energies in South Africa – they are there.

The liberation forces have been divided over a number of issues concerning revolutionary change in South Africa. On the one hand the PAC and the BCM have adopted a purely nationalist approach while on the other hand, the ANC and SACP movements have adopted a more socialist approach based around the notion of class. Yet an examination of the differences between the separate revolutionary and cultural struggles only serves to undermine the opportunity to capitalise on the South African crisis. I have argued that if this type of counter-hegemonic bloc is to materialise, solidarity involving forms of economic, political and cultural struggles must emerge. The destruction of apartheid requires a co-ordinated struggle not only through armed struggle, or national struggle, or class struggle, or through cultural struggle, but through the convergence of all forms of resistance and struggle, including sport.

APPENDIX 1

SOUTH AFRICAN DISPUTES INVOLVING BLACK WORKERS AT THE HEIGHT OF THE 1981 STRIKE WAVE

Date	Firm	Number	Union	Comment
1 July 1981	SASOL	1,000	BCAWU	Construction workers on oil refinery site deported to Bantust.
2 July 1981	Sea Harvest	900	FCWU	Reinstatement plus wage increase after sympathy strikes in other Saldanah Bay fish plants.
3 July 1981	Salcast	2,000	MAWU	Walk out over wages until negotiate.
3 July 1981	African Malleable Foundries	2,000	MAWU	Out for a day in support of negotiations (Benoni).
6 July 1981	Telephone manufacturers		MAWU	Protest at productivity impositions (Springs).
8 July 1981	Blackman & Co.	65	GWU	Reinstatement after one victimisation (Cape Town).

Date	Firm	Number	Union	Comment
8 July 1981	SA Cape Fellmongers	170		All sacked for supporting five victimised.
9 July 1981	Ilco Homes	2,000	SAAWU	Sacked for supporting fourteen (Durban).
13 July 1981	Anglo-American	10,000		Over death benefits of miners (in text).
13 July 1981	Vaal Metal	180	MAWU	Wage increase achieved (Boksburg).
13 July 1981	Raleigh Cycles		EAWU	Workers again elect for union representative.
13 July 1981	Gourmet Fish	80	FCWU	Parity strike with Saldana Bay (Helena).
14 July 1981	Colgate-Palmolive	500	CWIU	Protracted wage negotiations brought to speedy conclusion (Boksburg).
15 July 1981	Bosal Afrika		NUMARWOSA	Union recognised (Uietenage).
15 July 1981	Tensile Rubber		MAWU	Wage increases secured (Wynberg).
15 July 1981	Buffalo Salt	200	SFAWU	Walkout during pay talks. Industrial.

Appendix 1

Date	Firm	Number	Union	Comment
15 July 1981	Hendler	2,000	MAMU	Week's strike achieves increase (Boksburg).
16 July 1981		60		Warehouse-man fired for striking.
17 July 1981	Bisonbord	270	PWAWU	Reinstated over wage dispute (Boksburg).
17 July 1981	Langeberg Canning	1,300	FCWU	800 locked-out day shift joined by 500 night over wages.
20 July 1981	East Rand Mines	2,500		110 arrested and forty fired over wages.
24 July 1981	De Gama Textile	4,000	SAAWU	Ten detained during police picket attack.
27 July 1981	Plant Protection	68	CWIU	Reinstatement of two victimised (Brakpan).
28 July 1981	Freuhauf Trailer	400	MAWU	During wage negotiations (Wadeville).
29 July 1981	Piggot, Masket		CWIU	Recognition won (Boksburg).

Source: J. Rogers (1982), *Striking Against Apartheid*

APPENDIX 2

THE SOUTH AFRICAN GOVERNMENT'S OFFICIAL MULTINATIONAL SPORTS POLICY

In September 1976, Dr P.G.H. Koornhof, Minister of Sport, announced the basis of 'multinational' sport which remains government policy to this day.

The federal council accept that, taking into account the applicable legislation and regulations, the interests of South Africa and all its people in respect of sport can best be served in terms of the following policy:

1 That white, coloured, Indian and black sportsmen and women should all belong to their own clubs and that each should control, arrange and manage its own sporting fixtures;

2 That wherever possible, practical and desirable, the committees or councils of the different race groups should consult together or have such contact as would advance the interests of the sport concerned;

3 That intergroup competition in respect of individual types of sport be allowed at all levels, should the controlling bodies so decide;

4 That in respect of team sports, the councils or committees of each racial group should arrange their own leagues or programmes within the racial group;

5 That where mutually agreed, councils or committees may, in consultation with the Minister of Sport, arrange leagues or matches enabling teams from different racial groups to compete;

6 That each racial group should arrange its own sporting relationships with other countries or sporting bodies in accordance with its own wishes and that each should award its own badges and colours;

7 That if and when invited or agreed, teams comprising players from all racial groups can represent South Africa, irrespective of whether the type of sport is an Olympic sport

or not, and that such participants can be awarded badges or colours which, if so desired, can incorporate the national flag or its colours;

8 That attendance at sporting fixtures be arranged by the controlling bodies.

Source: R. Archer and B. Bouillon (1982), *The South African Game*

APPENDIX 3

SOUTH AFRICAN SPORTING HISTORY

1652	Importation of first horses.
1795–1802	Foundation of the first horse racing club.
1808	First recorded cricket match.
1854	Hottentot Boer cricket match.
1874	First football club.
1876	First rugby club established. First coloured and African cricket clubs.
1879	First athletics club. First cycling club.
1882	Formation of white rugby federation (SARB).
1890	White cricket federation formed (SACA).
1892	Formation of white football federation (FASA). Formation of white athletics association.
1896	Formation of first black rugby federation (SACRFB).
1899–1902	White swimming federation formed. Rugby match between Boer–British armies.
1908	White Olympic Committee formed (SACOEGA). South Africa participates for the first time in the Olympic Games.
1923	White hockey federation formed.
1938	Introduction of a national physical education programme.
1946	Non-Racial Table Tennis Board recognised by the international body.

1951	Multiracial football federation created (SASF).
1955	Blacks excluded from Bloemfontein Stadium.
1956	Non-Racial Table Tennis Board accorded exclusive recognition by international federation. Dr Donges's sports policy statement.
1958	South African Sports Association formed (SASA).
1960	Black federations make initial moves towards non-racialism. Several black federations affiliate with dependent status to white federations.
1962	SASF (football) and SACBOC (cricket) become non-racial; non-racial tennis union formed. Formation of the South African Non-Racial Olympic Committee (SAN-ROC).
1964	South Africa excluded from Olympic Games. SAN-ROC leaders harassed. Maoris refused visiting visas.
1966	SAN-ROC regroups in exile. Formation of non-racial swimming federation. Minister of Sport and Recreation appointed. South Africa excluded from Olympic Games. Basil d'Oliveira affair (cricket).
1967	Vorster statement on sport.
1970	South Africa expelled from Olympic movement. South African Non-Racial Sports Organisation formed (SASPO).
1971	Multinational sports policy statement. Dr Koornhof becomes Minister of Sport. South African Council on Sports (SACOS) formed.
1976	Multinational sports policy finalised. Gleneagles Agreement signed.
1979	Dr Klerk appointed Minister of Sport.
1979	New Non-Racial Tennis federation (TASA). Janson appointed specific Minister for Sport. Overall control of sport in all communities.
1980	British Sports Council fact finding mission. French sports delegation investigates South African sport.

Rhodesia cuts off sporting links with South Africa.
British Lions tour South Africa.
Argentina bans South African cricketers.

1981 Ireland tours South Africa (rugby).
Springboks tour New Zealand.
Springboks tour United States (Eastern Provinces).
English Football Coaching Tour.
Borg and McEnroe refuse to play in the South African Open.

1982 United Nations black list shows the UK and the USA to have the most sporting links with South Africa.
English Cricket Tour.
English Football Tour.
Sri Lankan Cricket Tour.
British and French invitation rugby select arrives in South Africa.

1983 West Indian rebel cricket tour.
French Rugby Union Tour cancelled.
MCC Tour cancelled.
Liverpool and Manchester United reject substantial offer to tour.

1984 English Rugby Union Tour.
Welsh Rugby Union maintain sporting links with South Africa.
Olympic resolution condemning apartheid.
Commonwealth Games Association critical of English Rugby Tour of South Africa.
The Zola Budd Affair.
South African Schoolboys rugby tour of Wales.

Source: Developed from R. Archer and B. Bouillon (1982), *The South African Game.*

NOTES

Introduction

1 For instance see Hain (1971), Lapchik (1975), Brickhill (1976).

2 The granting of British citizenship to the South African Zola Budd, unable to compete in the 1984 Olympics for her country of birth, and jumping the queue of those who had waited up to ten years for citizenship, caused a storm of protest.

3 This argument is very much in line with Slovo (1976) and a number of ANC members when they argue that for all the overt signs of race as the mechanism of domination in South Africa the origin and perpetuation of legal and institutional domination lies in the relationships of economic exploitation.

4 For a further discussion on Oppenheimer see Saul and Gelb (1981).

5 Since taking office in September 1978, Prime Minister Botha has attempted to direct the South African regime on a new course, placing national security and survival above all else.

6 In South African politics the relatively right-wing approach is called *verkramp* and its advocates *verkramptes* (meaning narrow-minded). The relatively liberal approach is called in Afrikaans *verlig* and its proponents *verligtes* (meaning open-minded).

Chapter 1

1 The term is taken from Stasiulis (1980) who argues that pluralist approaches to South Africa are characterised by institutional and ethnological determinism. The critique of pluralism which follows draws heavily from Stasiulis.

2 Work on the relationship between racial oppression and

capitalist exploitation by Wolpe (1972), (1983), Legassick (1974), and Johnstone (1976) provide useful examples of the Marxist analysis of South Africa.

3 Williams (1977) writing on human experience is reminiscent of the Marxian term 'praxis'.

4 Gramsci referred to these periods as periods of social transformation.

5 See Saul and Gelb (1981), Callinicos (1981), Wolpe (1983).

6 For such a differentiation see Boggs (1980: 116).

Chapter 2

1 The initial period of segregation dates back to 1841. However, it has been adopted and refined by the present-day rulers of South Africa as the most convenient system whereby Africans who are not directly contributing to white prosperity can be excluded from the rich zone and not become a burden upon its resources.

2 Translated the term 'No Sizwe' refers to the no-name author. At present the author, having spent many years on Robben Island, is currently living in exile, hence the 'no-name' name.

3 The 1936 Land Act established what were already *de facto* African reserves as a legal entity.

4 Figures from Saul and Gelb (1981).

5 Besides ISCOR (steel), IDC (the Industrial Development Corporation) and ESCOM (electricity), there are now also ARMSCOR (weapons), SASOL (oil from coal), FOSKOR (phosphorus) and SAPPI (pulp and paper), among others.

6 For a full account of this period see Callinicos and Rogers (1977).

Chapter 3

1 A number of the well-known accounts of South African sport have tended to over-emphasise the part played by sport in bringing about change in South Africa (Krotee and Schwick, 1979, Shaw and Shaw, 1977; Lapchick, 1975). What these accounts fail to realise is that when we are talking about change in sport in the South African case it is socio-economic change that we are talking about. Sport does not exist within a social vacuum.

2 In *Marxism Today* (September 1982) Bose makes the point that

when we are talking about South African sport we are primarily talking about western European forms of sport, i.e. white sport. Although indigenous forms of cricket like kabbadi are played in South Africa, it ranks so far below cricket that it virtually disappears when the cricket season starts.

3 What historical material does exist can be found in Archer and Bouillon, 1982 and Bose, 1982. The treatment of non-racial sport in the literature to date has mainly been in the context of the political sphere. The cultural significance of non-racial sporting forms has been ignored (Grace, 1974).

4 The period is broadly identified by a number of authors as lasting from 1867-1910 (Saul and Gelb, 1981; *Review of African Political Economy*, no. 7, London).

5 None more so than the game of rugby (Woods, 1981).

6 One such incident occurred during 1969–70 when Britain became the focal point of protest because of the proposed Springbok tour which had been planned for that year. The extent of the campaign was so great that the Labour government in 1970 made a formal request to the MCC to cancel the 1970 cricket test series with South Africa (Hain, 1971; Richards, 1978; Jarvie, 1981).

7 See Gruneau (1975, 1976) for analyses of Canadian sport in terms of social differentiation.

8 Between 1928 and 1933 white racial sporting federations were founded in rifle-shooting, motor-racing, and basketball.

9 On 15 June 1977 the government heads of Commonwealth countries met in London to sign a declaration condemning apartheid in sport. For full details see *Olympic Reviews*, no. 118, August 1977.

10 Quoted from a letter from Dennis Howell, MP, to the author dated 7 April 1978.

11 In criticism of multinationalism the United Nations pointed out the fraudulent character of this policy in that it obscured the fact that it was racist and colonialist, its sole purpose being to ensure the continuing political and economic domination of the white minority not only throughout the Republic of South Africa but also in unliberated parts of southern Africa as a whole (United Nations, *Objective Justice*, vol. 8, no. 1, Spring 1976).

12 See Poulantzas (1980), Giddens (1982), Miliband (1978).

13 See Cantelon and Gruneau (1982), for work on sport and the state.

14 Mainly through propaganda and refusal to participate in white-organised events, non-racial movements have attracted a considerable amount of attention to the weaknesses surrounding

multinational sport. Over twenty genuine non-racial sports disciplines have affiliated to SACOS (Ramsamy, 1982).

15 The official attitude towards Africans is that they should pay for their own social and community services from taxation, beer hall sales, licensing revenue, etc. This approach penalises the lowest paid for their poverty and cripples African education and housing as well as sport (Brickhill, 1976, Seidman, 1980; Plant, 1982).

16 Colgate-Palmolive has an annual budget of about R120,000 for the promotion of multinational sport. Barclays Bank provides annually in the region of R35,000 for cricket coaching. Datsun Nissan are regular sponsors of golf, cricket and football and British Petroleum are regular sponsors of football (Ramsamy, 1982).

17 The 1981 Springbok rugby tour has been viewed as an attempt by the Reagan administration to expand its growing alliance with South Africa. Similar negotiations were carried out in 1978 (Lapchick, 1979).

18 Commenting on Jimmy Hill's attempt to justify the South African soccer tour, Bose points out that the mythical bridge-building argument is often used. It claims that international tours are not so much for the whites but for the oppressed blacks and non-whites who will then appreciate what the world has to offer and will learn from it (Bose, 1982).

19 In October 1980 Southern Sun tried to persuade two top international tennis stars, John McEnroe and Bjorn Borg, to play a challenge match in Bophuthatswana. The two players were to share R900,000 with an extra R120,000 for the winner. The match was aborted because both players refused to provide apartheid with international respectability (*Rand Daily Mail*, 2 October 1980). In July 1982 the proposed soccer tour involving World Cup stars was cancelled because a number of players, including Mario Kempas and Osvaldo Ardilles, refused to participate (Toronto *Sunday Star*, 18 July 1982).

20 Sponsors often assist with the organisation, provide attractive prize money, take care of travelling, hotel accommodation, expenses, and provide special equipment. In recent years commercial sponsorship has begun to play an important role in providing inflated fees for overseas participants (*South African Digest*, 16 March 1979).

Chapter 4

1 In two conferences – one held in Kingwilliamstown in December 1975 and the other in Mafeking in May 1976 – the majority of BCM leadership formally outlined proposals for the kind of society it envisaged replacing the white apartheid state: a free Azania based on democratic elections, i.e. majority rule (No Sizwe, 1979).

2 In rejecting any analysis of contemporary South African society in terms of classes, Biko argued that Africans should think along such lines as 'buy black' and establish black community resources (Biko, 1979). Shortly after the Soweto uprising, Biko further declared that the BCM's objective was to build black power to a point where whites first had to listen.

3 For a full account of external resistance, see Lapchick, 1975 and 1978.

4 Middleton was the first President of SACOS.

5 Specific reference in this instance is made to those black Africans who co-opted into the multinational system.

6 By this I mean that the ANC's internal struggles regarding the place of nationalism or socialism within the broader liberation forces.

7 The Industrial Commercial Workers' Union (ICU), the first nationally based African workers' organisation, was founded in January 1919. Clements Kadalie became the first secretary of the union (see Wilkins, 1978).

8 See Eckstein (1965) for a discussion on the different contentions of revolutionary change.

9 The Freedom Charter which the ANC officially adopted in 1956, marked a shift in policy from the African nationalist position adopted during the 1940s. While the earlier programme of action had stressed the attainment of self-determination and political independence under the banner of African nationalism, the Freedom Charter glossed over the nationalist side of the liberation struggle.

10 While Brutus became the international symbol for non-racial sport Papwa Sewgolum became the first sporting martyr in the opposition to apartheid. Having won the Natal Open Golf Championship in January 1963, under the Group Areas Act, the player was not allowed to enter the clubhouse to receive his award (Lapchick, 1975; Archer and Bouillon, 1982; Ramsamy, 1982).

11 SAN-ROC's President lost his passport, and Secretary Reg Hlongwane had to flee abroad to avoid being banned. Denis

Brutus was arrested in 1963, while in 1965 former President John Harris was sentenced to death having been arrested for sabotage (see Hain, 1971; Lapchick, 1975; Ganga, 1979).

12 For details of Biko's death and inquest proceedings see Bernstein (1978).

13 During 1979 assassination attempts were made on the lives of SACOS Secretary M.N. Patner and Morgan Naidoo, President of the Non-Racial Swimming Federation.

14 The name of SACOS has become so closely associated with the struggle for non-racial sport that both within South Africa and outside the two have almost become confounded (Hunter, 1980).

15 See United Nations, 8/80.

16 See United Nations 8/80; Archer and Bouillon (1982).

17 Any member of a multinational or umbrella sporting organisation was automatically excluded from SACOS membership.

18 The argument is pursued in Callinicos (1981) where he argues that a socialist revolution must be the precondition of national liberation in South Africa, even if the development of consciousness among the black masses provides a stimulus to the formation of class consciousness. The point is also stressed in Hirson (1979).

19 By this I mean Fanon (1965, 1967, 1982).

20 Lenin's fixation on the conjunctural had a political as well as a theoretical impact, for it opened the door to a dangerous form of Jacobinism that would eventually negate the prospects for socialism (see Boggs, 1980).

21 See Chapter 1 for the way in which 'hegemony' is used in this study.

BIBLIOGRAPHY

Adam, H. (1971), *Modernising Racial Domination*, Berkley: University of California Press.

Adam, M. (1979), 'Ethnic mobilisation and the politics of patronage', *Ethnic and Racial Studies*, vol. 2, no. 2.

Archer, R. and Bouillon, B. (1982), *The South African Game*, London: Zed Press.

Aron, R. (1965), *Main Currents in Sociological Thought*, London: Basic Books.

Ashe, A. (1977), 'Thoughts on the Davis Cup and world politics', *World Tennis*, vol. 25, no. 2, July.

Banton, M. (1967), *Race Relations*, New York: Basic Books.

Barrell, H. (1980), 'A new phase of rebellion', *New Statesman*, June.

Bensob, M. (1966), *South Africa: The Struggle for a Birthright*, Harmondsworth: Penguin Books.

Berman, J. (1982), 'Black unions start winning', *New Statesman*, January.

Bernstein, H. (1978), *Steve Biko, No. 46*, London: International Defence and Aid Fund (IDAF).

Biko, S. (1979), *I Write What I Like*, London: Heinemann.

Boggs, C. (1970), *Racism and Class Structure*, London: Monthly Review Press.

Boggs, C. (1980), *Gramsci's Marxism*, London: Pluto Press.

Bose, S. (1982), 'Sport and South Africa', *Marxism Today*, September, vol. 26, no. 9.

Brickhill, J. (1976), *Race Against Race*, London: IDAF.

Brutus, D. (1972), 'The sportsman's choice', in La Guma, A. (ed.), *Apartheid: A Collection of Writings on South African Racism*, London: Lawrence & Wishart.

Caffrey, K. (1973), *The British to Southern Africa*, London: Gentry Books.

Callinicos, A. (1981), *Southern Africa After Zimbabwe*, London: Pluto Press.

Callinicos, A. and Rogers, J. (1977), *Southern Africa After Soweto*, London: Pluto Press.

Cantelon, H. and Gruneau, R. (1982), *Sport, Culture and the Modern State*, Toronto: University of Toronto Press.

Cardoso, F.H. (1972), 'Dependency and development in Latin America', *New Left Review*, no. 74.

Chilicote, R. (1974), 'Dependency: A critical synthesis of Literature', *Latin American Perspective*, vol. 1, no. 1.

Collins, J. (1980), *Southern Africa: Freedom and Peace*, London: IDAF.

Eckstein, H. (1965), 'On the etiology of internal wars', *History and Theory* 4, vol. 2.

Engels, F. (1980), 'Ludwig Feuerbach and the end of classical German philosophy', in Marx, K. and Engels, F., *Selected Works*, New York: International Publishers.

Fanon, F. (1965), *A Dying Colonialism*, New York: Grove Press.

Fanon, F. (1967), *Towards the African Revolution*, New York: Grove Press.

Fanon, F. (1982), *The Wretched of the Earth*, Ontario: Penguin Books.

Frank, André Gunder (1966), 'The development of underdevelopment', *Monthly Review*, vol. 17, September.

Frank, André Gunder (1967), *Capitalism and Underdevelopment in Latin America*, New York: Monthly Review Press.

Frank, André Gunder (1969), *Latin America: Underdevelopment or Revolution?* New York: Modern Reader.

Frank, André Gunder (1972), *Lumpen Bourgeoisie and Lumpen Development*, New York: Monthly Review Press.

Furnivall, J.S. (1948), *Colonial Policy and Practice*, London: Cambridge University Press.

Ganga, J. (1979), *Combats pour un sport Africain*, Paris: Harmattan.

Gerhart, G. (1978), *Black Power in South Africa*, Berkeley: University of California Press.

Giddens, A. (1980), *Capitalism and Modern Social Theory*, Cambridge: Cambridge University Press.

Giddens, A. (1982), *Sociology: A Brief but Critical Introduction*, London: Macmillan Press.

Grace, M. (1974), 'Origin and development of governmental sports policies in the Republic of South Africa', in *Proceedings of the North American Society for Sport History*, London, Ontario: Penn State University.

Gramsci, A. (1980), *Selection from Prison Notebooks*, New York: International Publishers.

Gruneau, R.S. (1975), 'Sport, social differentiation and social inequality', in D. Ball and J.W. Loy (eds), *Sport and Social Order*, London: Addison-Wesley.

Gruneau, R.S. (1976), 'Sport as an area of sociological study', in R.Gruneau and J. Albinson (eds), *Canadians' Sport: Sociological Perspectives*, Toronto: Addison-Wesley.

Gruneau, R.S. (1982), 'Sport and debate on the state', in H. Cantelon and R. Gruneau (eds), *Sport, Culture and the Modern State*, Toronto: University of Toronto Press.

Guma, A. La (1972), '*Apartheid: A Collection of Writings on South African Racism by South Africans*', London: Lawrence & Wishart.

Hain, P. (1971), *Don't Play with Apartheid*, London: Allen & Unwin.

Hain, P. (1979), 'Politics of sport in South Africa', *New Society*, vol. 50, no. 890.

Hall, S. (1981), 'Moving right', *Socialist Review*, no. 55.

Hall, S. and Jefferson, T. (1976), *Resistance Through Rituals*, London: Hutchinson.

Harsch, E. (1980), *South Africa: White Rule, Black Revolt*, New York: Monad Press.

Hirson, D. (1979), *Year of Fire, Year of Ash: Soweto Revolt*, London: Zed Press.

Humphrey, D. (1975), *Cricket Conspiracy*, London: National Council for Civil Liberties.

Hunter, M.G. (1980), 'United Nations are the anti-apartheid movement in sport' in *Canadians' Journal of History of Sport and Physical Education*, 11 (1) May.

Jarvie, G. (1981), 'The case of South Africa', in *Scottish Journal of Physical Education*, vol. 9, no. 1.

Johnson, R. (1979), 'Histories of culture/theories of ideology', in Barret *et al.*, *Ideology and Cultural Production*, London: Croom Helm.

Johnstone F. (1976), *Class, Race and Gold: A Study in Class Relations and Racial Discrimination in South Africa*. London: Routledge & Kegan Paul.

Karis, T. and Carter, G.N. (1972), *From Protest to Challenge*, vol. 3, Stamford, California: Hoover Institute Press.

Kay, G. (1980), *Development and Underdevelopment*, London: Macmillan Press.

Kidd, B. (1978), *Political Economy of Sport*, Toronto, Ontario: CAPHER.

Krotee, M. and Schwick, L. (1979), 'Impact of sporting forces on South African Apartheid', *Journal of Sport and Social Issues*, vol. 3, no. 1.

Kuper, L. (1965), *An African Bourgeoisie's Race, Class and Politics in South Africa*, New Haven: Yale University Press.

Kuper, L. and Smith, M.G. (1969), *Race, Class and Power*, Los Angeles: University of California Press.

Laclau, E. (1971), 'Feudalism and capitalism in Latin America', *New Left Review*, no. 67.

Lapchick, R. (1975), *The Politics of Race and International Sport*, Westport, Connecticut: Greenwood Press.

Lapchick, R. (1978), 'Negotiations with the United States Tennis Federation', *Journal of Sport and Social Issues*, vol. 2, no. 2.

Lapchick, R. (1979), 'Sports and apartheid politics', *Annals of the American Academy of Political and Social Science*, no. 445, September, 1979.

Lapchick, R. (1981), 'Access Report on the 1981 Springbok Tour of the USA', *Arena Review*, vol. 5, no. 3.

Legassick, M. (1974), 'Capital accumulation and violence', *Economy and Society*, vol. 3, no. 3.

Lenin, V.I. (1961), 'What is to be done?', *Collected Works*, vol. 5, Moscow: Progress Publishers.

Lenin, V.I. (1964), *Collected Works*, Vol. 22, Moscow: Progress Publishers.

Lenin, V.I. (1966), *Collected Works*, Vol. 31, Moscow: Progress Publishers.

Leys, C. (1976), *Unpublished Notes on Dependency*, Kingston: Queen's University.

Louw, J. (1977), *Sport and Race Relations in South Africa*, PhD Thesis: University of Alberta.

Luckhardt, K. and Wall, B. (1980), *Organise or Starve*, London: Lawrence & Wishart.

Lukes, S. (1974), *Power: A Radical View*, London: Macmillan Press.

Lukes, S. (1977), *Essays in Social Theory*, London: Macmillan Press.

Magubane, B. (1979), *Political Economy of Race and Class in South Africa*, New York: Monthly Review Press.

Mandela, N. (1978), *The Struggle is my Life*, London: IDAF.

Marx, K. and Engels, F. (1980), *Selected Works*, New York: International Publishers.

Miliband, R. (1978), *Marxism and Politics*, Oxford: Oxford University Press.

O'Meara, D. (1975), 'The 1946 African mineworkers' strike', *Journal of the Commonwealth and Comparative Politics*, vol. 13, no. 2, July.

Panitch, L. (1981), *Canadian Journal of Political Economy*, Winter 1981, no. 6.

Plant, M. (1982), *The Struggle for Southern Africa*, London: War and Want and Liberation.

Poulantzas, N. (1980), *Political Power and Social Classes*, London: New Left Books.

Ramsamy, S. (1982), *Apartheid: The Real Hurdle*, London: IDAF.

Richards, G. (1978), 'Report on New Zealand's implementation of the Gleneagles Agreement', in *Journal of Sport and Social Issues*, vol. 2, No. 2.

Rogers, B. (1980), *Divide and Rule*, London: IDAF.

Rogers, J. (1982), *Striking Against Apartheid*, London: Socialists Unlimited.

Saul, S. and Gelb, S. (1981), *The Crisis in Southern Africa*, London: Monthly Review Press.

Santos, D. (1970), 'The structure of dependence', *American Economic Review*, vol. 60 (May).

Seidman, J. (1980), *Facelift Apartheid*, London: IDAF.

Shaw, T. and Shaw, S. (1977), 'Sport as trans-national politics: A preliminary analysis of labour', *Journal of Sport and Social Issues*, vol. 1, no. 2.

Simon, R. (1982), *Gramsci's Political Thought*, London: Routledge & Kegan Paul.

Sivanadan, A. (1982), *Writings on Black Resistance*, London: Pluto Press.

Sizwe, No (1979), *One Azania: One Nation*, London: Zed Press.

Slovo, S. (1976), *Southern Africa: New Politics of Revolution*, Harmondsworth: Penguin.

Smith, M.G. (1960), 'Social and cultural pluralism', *Annals of New York Academy of Sciences*, vol. 83.

Sports Council (1980), *Sport in South Africa*, Sports Council Fact Finding Delegation.

Stasiulis, D. (1980), 'Pluralist and Marxist perspectives on racial discrimination in South Africa', *British Journal of Sociology*, vol. 21, no. 4, December.

Sunkel, D. (1972), 'Big business and dependency', *Foreign Affairs* (L) April.

Taljaard, E. (1981), 'Sport and recreation facilities in the Cape Province of the Republic of South Africa', *South African Journal for Research in Sport, Physical Education and Recreation*, vol. 4, no. 2.

Van den Berghe, P. (1965), *South Africa: A Study in Conflict*, Berkeley: University of California Press.

Van den Berghe, P. (1967), *Race and Racism*, New York: Willey & Sons.

Van den Berghe, P. (1969), *Race and Ethnicity: Essays in Comparative Sociology*, London: Basic Books.

Wilkins, P. (1978), *The Industrial and Commercial Workers' Union Of South Africa*, Oxford: Oxford University Press.
Williams, R. (1966), *Culture and Society*, Harmondsworth, Penguin.
Williams, R. (1976), *Keywords*, Glasgow: Fontana.
Williams, R. (1977), *Marxism and Literature* Oxford: Oxford University Press.
Williams, R. (1980), *Problems in Materialism and Culture*, London: Verso.
Williams, R. (1981), *Culture*, London: Fontana.
Willis, P. (1977), *Learning to Labour*, Westmead: Saxon House.
Wolpe, H. (1972), 'Capitalism and cheap labor power in South Africa', *Economy and Society*, vol. 1, no. 4.
Wolpe, H. (1983), 'Apartheid Rule', in *Marxism Today*, February.
Woods, D. (1981), *Black and White*, Dublin: Ward River Press.

Documentation and letters:

Letter from Denis Howell, MP, dated 7 April 1978.
Letter from Richard Lapchick, dated 27 October 1981.
Letter from Sam Ramsamy, dated 31 October 1981.
Letter from Denis Brutus, dated 6 January 1982.

United Nations Center Against Apartheid Official Report 8/80.

Hansard
25 May 1973.
4 June 1976.
18 May 1977.
21 May 1979.

The Sunday Times
9 December 1973.
2 January 1980.
26 February 1980.

Rand Daily Mail
6 April 1978.
2 October 1980.

Toronto Star
18 July 1982.

South African Digest
16 March 1979.

INDEX

Adam, H., 6, 9–12, 14
African Mine Workers Union, 29,
    42; the 1946 strike, 30–1
African National Congress, 36;
    sasol oil plant bombings, 38–9,
    63–4; split with PAC, 67–8, 69;
    strategy, 65–6, 73, 74
Archer, R. and Bouillon, B., 44–7,
    49, 57, 65, 67, 73, 86; South
    African sporting history
    88–90
Azanian African People's
    Organization, 64, 68, 73

Banton, M., 6
bantustan strategy, 27–30, 40–2
Bermen, J., 38
Biko, S., 35, 64–8, 96
Black Consciousness Movement,
    64; and nationalism, 73–5, 81;
    and Soweto, 68–9
black sporting history, 45–50,
    53–4, 65–6, 67–73; and
    hegemony 73–7
Boggs, C., 92, 96; on Gramsci's
    model at transformation, 21–7,
    76
Bose, M., 80, 92, 94
Botha, P.W., 5; legitimation of
    changes, 39, 41–3, 80;
    rationalizing apartheid, 7, 38
boycotts, 28–31, 35, 79; sporting

boycotts, 54, 65, 70–3, 80–2;
    Soweto riots, 36–8
Brickhill, J., 53, 54, 58, 68, 91,
    94
Brutis, D., 68

Callinicos, A., 29, 33–4, 40, 77,
    92, 96
capital: cheap labour, 10, 27–9;
    conflicting Dutch and British
    interests, 11, 27, 29, 31–2;
    process of capital accumulation,
    12–14, 26–33, 58–61; relations
    of production, 15–17
class: culture, 15–18, 46–7; and
    nation, 64–5, 73–4; and race,
    1–2, 6, 8–15; struggle, 1–3,
    12–24, 26–30, 34–9; through
    sport, 65–73, 75–7
colonization, 1–2, 26–7; and sport,
    45–7
communist party of South Africa,
    66, 73, 81
conjunctural, 3–5, 18; definition of,
    21, 23; response in South Africa,
    39–43; and sport, 43, 53–6, 64,
    78, 80
consciousness, 25, 34–8, 65, 79
cricket, 1, 45–7, 53–5, 58–60
crisis: economic, 3, 5, 32–4; or-
    ganic and conjunctural, 21–3,
    39–43, 53–6

105

culture: class, 15–18, 46–7; cultural pluralism, 7; cultural struggle, 73–7

Dutch East India Company, 26–7

education, 35, 36, 39, 50
Engels, F., 12
exile, 49, 53, 67–9

Fanon, F., 64, 74–5, 96
football, 46, 60
foreign investment, 2, 32–4, 42, 73, 79
freedom charter, 66
Furnivall, J.S., 7

Giddens, A., 16, 93
gold, 29, 31, 33, 79
golf, 60
Gramsci, A.: on hegemony, 18–21; on the organic and conjunctural dimensions of crisis, 21–3; on revolutionary theory, 21, 24, 75–6; on the role of intellectuals, 20
Group Areas Act, 61–2

Hain, P., 51, 91, 93, 96
Hall, S., on hegemony, 21; on the organic and conjunctural, 4, 23
Harsch, E., 32–4; on political consciousness, 35, 37
hegemony, 1–3; Gramsci's concept, 18–21; and sport, 48, 64, 73–7, 82; William's concept, 21
horse racing, 45, 47
Howa, H., 60

ideology, 1, 5, 6, 9, 58, 68, 78, 80
imperialism, 2, 32, 46
industrial action, 3, 25, 28, 30, 36–8, 68, 74, 79
Industrial Conciliation Act, 80

International Olympic Committee, 54, 68

Kadalie, C., 66
Karis, T., 66
Kidd, B., 15
Koornhof, Dr P., 1, 5, 39, 51–5
Kuper, L., 6, 8

labour movement: cheap labour, 26–8; history of struggle, 25–39, 68
land: formation of native reserves, 27–9, 30, 40
Lapchick, R., 51, 91, 92, 94
Legassick, M., 13, 92
Lenin, V., 76
liberal critique of pluralism, 9–11
liberation movement, 6, 63, 64, 65–6, 73–5, 80–2
Luckhardt, B., 29, 30, 34, 40
Lukes, S., 20

Magubane, B., 6, 13; cheap labour, 27–9
Mandela, N., 66
Marx, K., 12, 13–14; class struggle, 15–18; reserve army of labour, 28
Miliband, R., 93
mining, 29, 31, 32, 33
Multinational Sports Policy, 5, 45, 62, 80, 86,87; evolution of a sports policy, 52–5

national party, 23, 31, 47, 55
nationalism, 73–5, 81
Native Lands Act, 29, 30
native reserves, 27–9, 30, 40, 42

O'Meara, D., 30

Pan Africanist Congress, 64, 67, 73, 74, 75, 81
Plant, M., 41–2

pluralism, 7–9; critique of, 9–15
political economy of sport, 44–63
pragmatism, 10, 11

race, 1, 2; liberal position, 9–12;
pluralism, 7–9; and sport,
50–63, 64–72
Ramsamy, S., 60, 61, 62, 94, 95
Reservation of Separate Amenities
Act, 61–2
Rieckert Commission, 39, 40, 41,
84
Rodgers, B., 26
Rodgers, J., 83–5
rugby, 1, 46–7, 54, 59–60, 72

Saul, S. and Gelb, S., 6, 31, 32, 33,
34, 37, 68, 91
Seidman, J., 6, 57, 94
Sharpeville, 3, 29, 31, 56, 67, 79
Simon, R., 22
Sizwe, N., 27, 28, 31, 67, 92, 95
Slovo, S., 26, 91
Smith, M.G., 7, 8
South African Congress of Trade
Unions, 2, 41
South African Council on Sport,
49, 52, 60; resistance through
sport, 65–73; sport and
hegemony, 75–7, 81

South African Non-Racial Olympic Committee, 48, 64; resistance through sport, 65–73;
sport and hegemony, 75–7, 81
South African Sports Association,
48; resistance through sport, 65–
73; sport and hegemony, 75–7,
81
South African Student
Organization, 35
Soweto, 3, 25, 36–38, 56, 68, 79
sponsorship, 56, 58, 59, 71

table tennis, 48, 53
Taljaard, E., 58
Tiro, R., 35

Van den Berghe, 6; on pluralism,
8–10
Van Riebeeck, J., 26
verkramptes, 23, 91
verligtes, 5, 23, 56, 91
Vorster, B.J., 49, 53–4

Wiehahn Commission, 39, 40, 41,
80
Williams, R., 1–3; class struggle
and cultural production, 15–18;
on hegemony, 21
Wolpe, H., 92
Woods, D., 54, 93